THE ART OF DYING

Other Books by Salli Rasberry:

Living Your Life Out Loud

Running a One-Person Business

Marketing Without Advertising

Honest Business

The Seven Laws of Money

Rasberry Exercises

THE ART OF DYING

Honoring & Celebrating Life's Passages

Salli Rasberry and Carole Rae Watanabe

Celestial Arts
Berkeley • Toronto

"For This Journey" is from the collection of poems that first appeared in *Washing the Stones*. Maude Meehan. Reprinted by permission of the author.

"The Coffin Garden" essay previously appeared in *Saltwater Sweetwater* published by Floreant Press. © 1998 Salli Rasberry. Reprinted with permission from the editor.

Taking Risks previously appeared in *Living Your Life Outloud*. © 1995 Salli Rasberry and Padi Selwyn. Reprinted by permission of the authors.

CELESTIALARTS

P.O.Box 7123
Berkeley, California 94707

Celestial Arts titles are distributed in Canada by Ten Speed Canada, in the United Kingdom and Europe by Airlift Books, in South Africa by Real Books, in Australia by Simon & Schuster Australia, in New Zealand by Southern Publishers Group, and in Singapore, Malaysia, Hong Kiong and Thailand by Berkeley Books.

Cover and text design by Greene Design

Printed in the United States of America

Library of Congress Cataloging-in-Publication Data on file with the publisher

1 2 3 4 5 6 7 - 06 05 04 03 02 01

～ For Sasha Harrison
&
Tobin Yelland

∾ ACKNOWLEDGMENTS

Heartfelt thanks to all those who took time out from their lives to share their stories that were sometimes painful and always important. Your stories are the heart of this book.

Endless gratitude to Padi Selwyn, colleague and joy buddy, who helped lay the foundation for this book. For your contributions, stories, interviews, tears, and laughter—thank you sweetie!

Many thanks to my walking partners, Nancy Rowinsky, Miriam Redstone, and Jill Goffstein, who for five years patiently lived through all of the incarnations of this book, offering insight and support. Special kudos to Jill, the queen of rituals, for all of her work on rituals and ceremonies.

Thank you to Sasha Harrison, who typed all of the interviews, and to Mary Reid, who gave encouragement through all the rough parts. You continually brighten my life with your generous spirit. Thanks also to Karen Leonard, who knows more about death than any living person, and to Judy Tilt, who understands how to live with grace.

Thanks to Farley W. Wheelwright, who taught me about adjectives and so much more, to Robert Kourich, in whose garden the idea for this book emerged, and who, for many years, has been my fellow traveler in the sometimes challenging world of book publishing. Thank you to Willis Eschenbach, who rescued me from computer hell on more than one occasion, and to Michael Eschenbach, who sings all my favorite songs with gusto and is a wonderful dancer to boot.

Blessings upon our suberb editor, Veronica Randall, and David Charlsen who is always in my heart. And finally, to Wat, the Guardian Angel of Art Heaven.

∾ CONTENTS

Our desire in writing this book is to bring forth a more complete vision of death. It is time to invite death out of the shadows of the underworld into the sunlight of our lives, to open death's door and replace fear and denial with joy and freedom.

There is a renaissance under way. In the last twenty or so years, across our nation self-reliant and creative people have handcrafted their own wedding ceremonies, taken control of how and where their children were birthed, and are now redefining death and dying.

We hope to inspire and encourage more of you so that we are not just isolated pockets of people celebrating life/death, but are part of a greater spiritual awakening. One of the consequences of our modern, technological age is that we have become isolated from each other, from life and from death. The choice is ours—to remain disconnected onlookers or to seize the opportunity to become active advocates for more compassion and meaning in our lives.

Fear of death cripples us and keeps us from fully enjoying life, robbing us of our authenticity and condemning us to dwell only on the surface. We have to make ourselves accessible to the messages of death. This awareness creates the urgency to live our lives in a potent, beautifully crafted manner. Without it, our souls die of starvation. Death needs to be included in the banquet of life, because the art of living and the art of dying are inseparable. It's the conscious awareness of death throughout our lives that acts as a catalyst to live our lives with more magnificence.

We have not always been so separate from death. To the pioneers that settled this country, death was a constant companion and their children grew up accepting death as a natural, normal part of life. It was around the turn of the twentieth century that funeral professionals began to take over the functions of the family with regards to the dead, and procedures replaced natural impulses. As hospitals spread across the nation and medical technology flourished, the sick and the dying were no longer cared for at home. Gradually death was no longer considered a part of life.

To live the fullest lives possible we must reclaim the natural ways. To do this, we must first open up the conversation about death. We must speak honestly about death right along with the other passages that occur throughout our lives. These major periodic transformations, or shake-ups, are all part of the journey leading to the final passage.

In this book you will find practical wisdom and authentic ceremonies to celebrate these passages and to help you explore the rich possibilities of your life while demystifying the fear of change and death. We believe you will find yourself deepening, as you discover new possibilities for your life as you begin to live your freedom.

Collaboration

Carole and I have discovered our highest expression and profound joy through collaboration, and we find it especially valuable as we explore the connection between the art of living and dying. Adventuring together in the land of such strongly held taboos and facing our fears have opened our hearts in ways we couldn't have done alone. This book is a true collaboration. Each of us offers our most intimate gifts to the creation of this book.

Instead of identifying and keeping track of who did or said what, we decided to write in the first person. We have devoted ourselves to The Art of Dying—made a coffin garden, created art works, built a death castle, made altars, designed workshops, dreamed words and images, devoured books, and interviewed hundreds of people to bring you this offering. The exploration of death has greatly enriched our lives, and we want to share what we've learned.

Our hope is that you won't just read the words we've written here but will be willing to invest practice time, to take more risks with creative solutions, and to be open to fully experience the changes life demands of you. We have gathered many tools for transformation to help you deal with the big changes as they appear. To help stimulate your creativity we offer you potent rituals, models, stories, and guidelines to help you embrace death's release and to live life with stronger intention.

We are all learning together. Join us as we gain a deeper awareness of the scary, wondrous, mysterious inner world, where we will discover the gifts that death holds for us. Death—the spiritual part of life.

CHAPTER ONE

The Big Changes

Nature is, of course, the greatest proponent of change. The changing seasons reflect that there is no such thing as the permanent death of anything. There is a change of form and then a new life that comes forward every spring. In the garden, weeds, spent flowers, leaves, prunings from the orchard, and kitchen waste are transformed into compost to help feed the soil for next year's crop. This outer landscape has many similarities to the inner landscape of human emotions and feelings; they are always in flux, always contracting and expanding. Change is inherent in every human life. As Helen Nearing puts it in *Loving and Leaving the Good Life*, "To have partaken of and to have given love is the greatest of life's rewards. There seems never an end to the loving that goes on forever and ever. Loving and leaving are part of the living."

Most of us have never been taught to go through life's changes with awareness and intention. For most of us, change just seems to happen. It is as if we are tossed randomly from wave to wave. Sometimes we experience the exhilaration of catching a wave and riding it, but sometimes we are slammed unceremoniously onto the shore. How we navigate change forms the quality of our life and death. It determines our personal odyssey. Because life is a spiral and there is no way to know what lies ahead, it is prudent to live life with the awareness that change always happens. Embracing the challenge of change is a practice that will strengthen and help prepare you for the next change that is in the making.

During your lifetime you will go through many transitions. When you cross the bridges of change often enough you learn to recognize the road signs. The more aware you are with major transitions, the more at ease you will be in death. I have a Buddhist friend who prays for the adversity of small changes so he can develop his psychic muscles for the inevitable big changes.

Going through any life change, down to the simplest changes in personal habits, is a test of our ability to let go of the familiar. Life proceeds, and as we encounter challenges and surmount them we build confidence. It is our backlog of change and growth that allows us to face the ultimate change of death with the hope that we can die easily and with a sense of fulfillment.

Wonderful as it is to mark the high times in our lives, it is equally important to mark the difficult challenges in life, whether it is the loss of a job, ill health, an accident, or the end of a relationship. Because we don't have rituals for these events, we often feel shame or embarrassment during difficult times and then tend to hide our pain and anger by isolating ourselves. Slowly and surely more people across the country are beginning to realize the benefit of rituals during the hardest times. I hope during times of loss and difficulty that you will create rituals that will be authentic to you.

While you are going through hard times it may be difficult to believe that the negative things that are happening in your life are actually for your benefit. If your initial reaction is to fight and struggle and kick and scream, you are not alone. The most challenging lesson life has to teach is that change is constant and that we are not in control of it. We are, however, in control of our reaction to change and our willingness to be fully available to life. If you practice trying to use the experience and understand that 'this too will change,' change takes on a new dimension. I am not talking about the "you needed this lesson" or "you created your accident" perspective, which is irritating at best, but the philosophical idea that while change is happening, pay attention and use it as a point of growth and a point of departure to enter a new phase of life. You can transform loss by remaining open and looking forward instead of clinging to what was or what might have been. To find the rare gifts adversity has to offer, take the lid off of your curiosity and explore possibilities you've never before entertained. This can be your most important work during a time of struggle.

Anne Hill, author of *Circle Round, Raising Children in Goddess Tradition*, teaches her children about the impermanence of life and wrote this poem to help her family through their grief.

El Dia de Los Muertos
Wrap his little body in black silk,

reach down the damp hole

shoulder deep—place him there,

where the roots of oaks gather

to suck in the cold. The roses,

short-stemmed, go in next, with

stones that sound of the ocean.

Tell the children to get a piece

of candy, a teething toy, and they

do, though he never had teeth at all.

Push the dirt in, first with little hands

then bigger ones, pat it down as acorns

fall onto knuckles and laps. A stone,

gray as the body beneath, marks

the place like a navel, and marigolds

are scattered over earth and rock,

sinking like embers from the sun.

At last, now, in the cold blue air,

a new voice rattles the leaves,

then rises like smoke

through the veil of the day,

into the world's cradle.

This past year I felt stuck, not knowing what direction to go in. My work suddenly seemed too bright, too frivolous, that it no longer mirrored what I felt inside. I felt strangled and yearned for some heroic event to rescue me. I was experiencing the death of a certain phase of my life and art.

A natural progression and growth was beginning, but it felt like a large chunk of myself was falling away. The stretch of coastline I knew and loved was being replaced by an emptiness. There was nothing wrong with the painting I used to do, nothing wrong with me. I was simply changing. After several months of unsatisfying paintings, I knew I had to go through the fire and move to a new level. I spent the day painting through this dilemma with my mentor, Alice. The words 'Dignity' and 'Die Alive' appeared on a very dark, intense painting. The spell of anxiety was broken and my fear was replaced with a palette of deeper, richer colors and an aliveness that made me tremble. I knew by my sense of exhilaration that the needed shift had occurred.

Even though I have immersed myself in the subject of death, I still get terrified, especially when I contemplate life without those people who form the legs on my chair. I have suffered the death of people I love and have been near death myself. Each time another facet of myself has been revealed, and I have come to understand that "this too will pass." This doesn't mean I don't suffer incredibly or that I have hardened my heart with platitudes.

It is common for people to grow or shave a beard, choose a new hairstyle, or pick a new name when they are going through a transition. This is a conscious or unconscious signal that change is occurring. Others smash, break, burn, bury, or cut something to symbolize the end of a relationship or other big change. Or they go on retreat, fast, build a shrine, or any number of actions to mark an important passage. Less common, but growing in popularity, is the conscious creation of rituals that facilitate letting go of the old, embracing the new, and having that change witnessed within community.

Suzanne Arms, well known author of *Bestfeeding: Getting Breastfeeding Right for You* and many other books on birthing and midwifery, was planning a visit from Durango, Colorado. She wanted a group of her women friends to watch a videotape of her current project.

Impulsively I offered my house to her and found myself in a last minute whirlwind of house cleaning. A few minutes before my guests were to arrive, I was rummaging through my silverware drawer in search of a can opener when I came upon a very rusty paring knife. I didn't want my guests to see that neglected little knife, but I also didn't want to throw it in the trash where someone might get hurt, so I tossed it under the silverware tray and closed the drawer.

It was one of those foggy Northern California evenings and the atmosphere was intimate and cozy. Suzanne invited us to perform a ritual that she borrowed from Angelis Ariens, an anthropologist who has studied cultures all over the world.

First Suzanne asked us to choose an aspect of our lives we were ready to let go of. As we gathered around the butcher block in my kitchen, Suzanne asked if I had a knife that I was willing to sacrifice. Immediately I remembered that rusty little knife hidden in my kitchen drawer.

One by one we passed the knife, and Suzanne asked each of us: "What in your life is something that holds you back? What is it that you want to cut away that would then allow you to come more fully into your authentic self?"

After each woman spoke we responded by saying "oh," to show we heard her and to give support. When it was my turn my throat was extremely dry, and it was hard to get the words out. I realized how deeply I had buried my voice, how I had allowed myself to be smothered in the affairs of others and ignored my own work; denied my own song. Holding that little knife tightly, I closed my eyes and began to breathe deeply. As I affirmed out loud to the rest of the group my resolve to take back my power, to do my own work, warmth spread over my body and my voice emerged loud and firm and strong.

When we finished speaking the room seemed to vibrate with our power. Our ritual was not over, however, because we still needed to discard, in a symbolic way, whatever previously held us back. We formed a procession out into the misty night and together buried that rusty little knife beside a rock in the garden.

Anne Stine, a psychotherapist for more than twenty years, is the founder and director of Wilderness Rites. She leads groups dedicated to the natural unfoldment of cross-cultural rites of passage and wilderness quests in connection with the earth's cycles. Her work is an inspiration and she graciously shared some ideas with me for those that cannot, or do not choose to go on a quest at this time but want to learn how to grow through change consciously.

"The wilderness quest invites the person to go all the way through a particular change that he or she is in and to come out the other side," Anne explains. "The subtitle for this journey is 'dying practice.' I join together the idea of the process of change and transformation with our natural connection with earth and her cycles into the experience of dying practice. It is an ancient rite of passage that ritualizes life's transitions in a meaningful way and in solitude on the earth. It is a deep calling within the heart to leave one's daily life and return back to the earth for renewal, guidance, and clarity as one's self is reflected in the natural environment. Each quester returns empowered by her own way, which becomes her gift back in her life and community.

"There's no outer authority in the wilderness quest. What's inside the individual is where the authority and wisdom come from. As a ceremony this process gives people an opportunity to consciously, and with intention, go through a change and practice letting go. People are afraid to leave their families and all that's familiar behind. On the wilderness quest they don't take any of their 'stuff' with them. They only take what they have harvested, what I call self-love. Death also has to do with what people have to leave behind. On the wilderness quest people really get to see how they are going to be when the moment of death comes.

"There is a dying to the old that has to take place in change and an invitation to allow the new to come in.

"Everybody has something that is a challenge. Built into this ceremony of dying practice is the idea that there is always an ordeal to go through. Ceremony and ritual helps to make meaning out of the ordeal and assists us to go through them."

Contact information about Wilderness Rites is in the Resource section in the back of this book

Sometimes we are able to use a big life change to make the transition lightly into a brand new phase of life. If you have created a really stable basis for yourself, even in the midst of chaos it's possible to summon the confidence to make a leap into the future. Without a stable base, you may be pulled along dragging your heels, clutching frantically to what was, and resisting the next stage of your life. The quality of change has a lot to do with your attitude, with whether you can surrender and let go of the illusion of control, while remaining open and fostering a quiet, listening mind. The path of most vulnerability is the path of most growth, yet, as you live through the challenge of change, fear often eclipses your best intentions. It takes a lot of practice and faith to let go of what's old and familiar and keep in mind that change is going to occur whether you like it or not. *Change* happens.

My friend Judy is an inspiration and my mentor of death. She has taught me a lot about living through loss while keeping an open heart for what the future may bring.

One day I was helping Judy make some stepping stones out of pieces of handpainted tile and broken pottery for the entryway to her orchard. She told me this wonderful story about the orchard, her beloved husband Joe, and change as a part of healing. Twelve years earlier, Joe and Judy moved to a small apple farm in a semi-rural setting north of San Francisco. Joe particularly loved the orchard. It symbolized his desire to be a country farmer. He loved all the varieties of apples and how they grew and how tasty they were. Listening to Joe one would have thought he tended a million acres of trees.

Between the pool and the apple orchard stood a five foot laurel hedge, thick and impenetrable after many years of growth. Guests often asked, "Why the hedge?" since it blocked the view of the orchard and the hills beyond. Some even suggested that it should be cut down. Joe insisted that it hid some ugly wire fencing around the vegetable garden, and anyway, "It's always been there."

After much bargaining and pleading to make a cut in the hedge looking out toward the orchard, Joe finally acquiesced, but before Judy got around to it, Joe was tragically killed in an automobile accident.

Judy's son eventually cut an opening in the hedge, and Judy later decided that she wanted an arbor to frame the space. She commissioned a beautiful seven-foot, handcrafted arbor of twisted wrought iron with apples, leaves, and clusters of apple blossoms adorning the top. Judy dedicated it to Joe. Now from the house, from the pool, or from under the arbor, you can look out and see the funky fence around the vegetable garden and the climbing rose that Joe planted on it. There are sunflowers and ripening tomatoes in the vegetable garden where Joe loved to work, and beyond are the apples hanging heavily in the orchard where his ashes are scattered. It has become a path of remembrance for Joe's family and friends. Especially his wife.

Change can be empowering and inspiring. It can be a bridge allowing you to cross over to another place that you would not necessarily have chosen. The more you shield or insulate yourself from change and try to keep it from happening, the more your life shrinks into endless repetition and shallowness.

But it takes courage to allow the old to be discarded or consumed and the new to be born. It's not unlike that point when the trapeze artist lets go of the bar and reaches to grab the next one. Like the trapeze artist you have to trust that the next bar will be there, otherwise you won't get to reach out and experience the thrill of entering the next phase.

Change, like the loss of a job, can make you tentative and insecure and keep you from exploring new possibilities. Suppose that after many years with the same company you lose your job. After the initial shock, take a deep breath and try to view this change as a self-rousing opportunity.

Most importantly, let others know what's going on with you so they have the opportunity to help. Although you may not be comfortable with your new situation and are not yet at ease navigating an unfamiliar ocean, if you look around you will find help.

You might start interviewing people who have jobs that always interested you. If your finances allow, you could travel to another city where prospects might be better or take a vacation to clear your mind and gain a new perspective.

During times of unpleasant or particularly difficult change, the tendency for most of us is to either put on the happy face of denial or wallow around in the straight jacket of self-pity. Instead, try casting a wider net by opening your mind to new ideas, the support of friends, and unexpected insights that will allow you to transcend the usual restraints of the here and now and start you thinking about the future whatever it may bring.

If you keep expecting specific outcomes that don't happen, it becomes nearly impossible to believe in your own strength and ability to go through change. You will narrow your options and seek what is familiar and comfortable. Ask for help. Allow your friends to come through for you when you really need them. Isolation is the worst thing you can do to yourself during times of major change.

Take baby steps. Don't try to do too much at once. When you take one baby step at a time toward whatever the future holds and sincerely acknowledge each step, the getting there turns into a challenge that makes you a stronger person. Strong connections with friends create a safety net that will be there in the event of a big change. And remember—to get a friend you have to be a friend. A big part of weaving your safety net is to care for your closest friends. If you don't have your support system in place, there is no better time than today to begin. This net will support you when facing your own death or when you need soothing arms to hold you when your mate, parent, child, or close friend dies.

Tools for Transformation

You can create a variety of tools to help you through the big changes. For example, personal shrines, power houses, mask making, journaling, art, music, dance, rebirth, and self-love parties to name a few.

Shrines

I imagine you already have a shrine in your life; you just might not call it that. Your shrine might be framed photos of your family above the mantelpiece with candles on either side that you light on special occasions. Perhaps it's your car that you wax and shine and decorate with little sayings stuck to the dashboard or on the bumper. There might be a shrine on your kitchen windowsill, on top of your computer, or on your dresser—anywhere at all.

A personal shrine can also be a tool for assisting with change, helping you tap into the powerful ally of your unconscious. It can help you reconnect with the mystery of the universe and your forgotten wisdom. It can make the invisible visible. Your shrine enables you to go to a deeper level where you can connect with your power. This shrine is a place for personal ritual and can connect you to a still point where you can create something full of meaning for yourself. Creating a meaningful life uses the same principles as preparing for an empowering death.

A shrine is not necessarily static but can be an ongoing, changing expression that helps keep passion alive. Through words and objects you place on your altar, you make visible something inside your heart that is important to you and that can't be expressed in any other way. A shrine can be just for you or it can be a way of communicating with others who come into your world. Tending a shrine can be a beautiful way to bring a spiritual practice into your life. It is also a way to connect with those you love and even the larger community as well.

You can make a shrine from anything. You can take a piece of silk and write on it what you are wanting to move towards or what you are leaving behind and attach it to your shrine. You might include a small mirror. You can cut a simple house shape out of wood and make hinged doors so you can open and close your shrine. You might have two hooks at the top where you can hang a piece of canvas that you write or paint on, adding new layers when needed. Once you have gone through a change you can put the next piece of canvas on top or remove it and put it in your journal. You can put it in a place of honor or a special place where you feel comfortable and at peace.

Your shrine might be a cardboard box or a handcrafted one lined with velvet. Elaborate or simple, a shrine will become the place to act out, ritualize, and honor the most important passages of your life. This ritual space can be kept very private, or you can invite others to witness your changes, freeing yourself to go on to the next phase of growth.

When Judy's husband of many years died in a car accident, she created an altar to help her come to terms with his death.

As we sit in Judy's kitchen, a room full of sunlight, flowers, and treasures collected from their many travels, she showed me the small wooden altar she had painted in shades of orange, green, and yellow to honor Joe. There were roses and hearts painted on the sides and a picture of Our Lady of Guadalupe on the back. Judy placed a weeping angel figure inside, along with several heart-shaped rocks she had picked up on a beach in Mexico earlier that year. Sun-washed shells and bits of sea glass spilled out and mingled with votive candles for lighting at night. There was also a photo of an impromptu cairn of shells and stones made as she walked their favorite beach.

There was much joy as well as sadness in that room. Judy's smile was in her eyes one moment and the next moment her eyes filled with tears. This seemed natural and allowed me to feel comfortable talking about Joe, allowed me to reach out to Judy instead of tiptoeing around the fact that her husband was no longer there. She allowed her vulnerability to show along with her growth as she moved into the next stage in her life. The altar helped friends and family talk openly with Judy. Judy tells me: "It's important to put it out on the table, to be able to talk about my feelings with other people. And to remember."

Rituals to Make Change

Let me tell you about my friend Paula's forty-seventh birthday ritual. This was a pivotal year for her. She was a devoted mother of three teenagers, with two of her children headed off to college.

Twelve of Paula's closest women friends gathered for a surprise party in her honor. Before she arrived we made forty-seven candlestick holders out of clay that we placed around the room and on a large central table in a spiral. The spiral is a significant symbol as each of us keep traveling the same road but on different levels. This ritual was designed to celebrate Paula's current stage along her path.

The candles were placed in groups of ten, and as she lit the first group, Paula told of her birth and her earliest family memories and about her ancestors. The next ten candles represented Paula coming into her teen years and becoming a young woman. The lighting of the candles continued as she told of the wild and crazy times before she married, then falling in love with her husband, and the joys and challenges of motherhood. Whenever she spoke of times that involved any of us, we added our stories.

We held the ritual at night, and the ceremony began with the room in darkness. At the end when all the candles were finally lit, we told Paula how much light she has brought into the room and into our lives. This was a dynamic ritual. What a wonderful gift it was to all of us as we got to see a more total picture of our friend and to reflect on the importance of supporting and staying connected with each other. How wonderful it was to honor a friend in this way while she is still alive and we could all celebrate together.

Power Houses

One type of a shrine that I find useful in helping to make a positive life-change is the power house. The purpose of the power house is to help you create and visualize important goals in your life by providing a private place for concentrating on your dreams.

Begin by sitting quietly and listening to your inner voice—the one that speaks the truth about what's important to you. The voice of wisdom comes from instinct and insight often hidden behind the "shoulds" of everyday life. The trick is to get your talkative mind to hush long enough to pay attention. I usually hear my voice of wisdom while riding in my car alone, sitting quietly in meditation, rocking the cat in front of the fire, or washing the dishes. Next find or make a symbolic object that represents your personal goal and makes it tangible. You may want to include in your power house inspiring words that state your intention for change.

There was a time in my life when I was neglectful of myself. My neck was giving me lots of problems and my energy was lower than usual. When people asked how I was, I would tell them about my daughter, my grandchildren, my husband's business, my environmental work, but nothing really about me. Eventually I grew tired of neglecting my own needs, so I made a personal power house. In it I placed an alabaster bust of a graceful woman with a long neck. I also included a blue swan made out of glass and a strong African female figure carved from stone. I placed these objects along with a small bouquet of red and pink roses on top of a silk scarf. Then I wrote in bold marking pen the words written by Rachel Carlson: "This particular instant of time, that is mine." I placed fresh flowers and lit candles in my power house every day and within two weeks my life felt back in balance.

There are no hard and fast rules about making your power house, only that it be made with intention. You may have any number of objects in it—whatever feels right and helps you focus. This practice is much more about feeling than about thinking.

When I create a power house I do so with hope. For me it is an important tool for moving from one reality to the next. When you take your goals and visions seriously enough to make a power house you often include those around you in the magic of creating meaningful change. Your support system will help you make the goals happen in ways you can't know at this point. In the case of my near death experience with Lyme disease, I created a power house near my bed and used it to house the words and symbolic images that helped guide me through a difficult time. At one point when I was partly paralyzed and unable to speak I managed to write on the wall, "If I live I will only do my dreams." I listed my dreams in order of importance. Number one was to paint in France where the light would make me well. That dream helped me trade in the small vision of my bedroom and disease for a complete new lifestyle, where I now paint and teach in a house I bought in France, meeting students and friends who enrich my life in ways I had never dreamed possible.

Acknowledge Yourself

The most important tool in your life toolbox is personal trust or self-love. One way to build self-love is to meet a challenge and then acknowledge your achievement, especially in a public way. Take photos of your shrines and power houses and keep them in a special box. Look through your photos from time to time because they will tell the story of how you are building your life.

If you have friends who are doing the same practices and celebrations, it's fun to share your photos on special occasions. Bring them to an All Hallows Eve celebration where you and your friends can acknowledge and support each other. Make it a yearly celebration of each other's personal changes.

A fun way to mark change is to decorate a chair and set it aside for extraordinary occasions such as getting a degree, giving birth to a book, changing a career, winning a race, or letting go of a negative relationship. Let your imagination soar as you create your special chair. It may be a throne lavishly decorated in velvet and rhinestones. You might paint a wooden chair in your favorite colors—or cover a divan or a self-love seat. Anything goes. If you are generous you might let others sit in your chair on special occasions. Consider having a queen or king for a day party in your honor and enjoy it all from your special chair.

My dear friend, Delia Moon, decided to have a party to celebrate all of her dreams coming true. She was fifty-six, her children were grown and doing well, and she had become a grandmother. She had recently received her Master's degree in psychology, and two intentional communities she had been associated with for thirty years were flourishing. Life was very, very good.

Delia invited the most important people in her life to a catered sit-down dinner in her honor. There were two hundred people! Her family and friends seldom dressed up, so on the invitation she wrote, "Be as formal as you dare." There was an astonishing array of formal attire. One guest came all in sequins, another in a top hat. Delia engaged a flautist and a harpsichordist to play during the candlelit dinner and tears flowed as tribute after tribute was paid to her. A "git down" rhythm and blues pianist provided music for dancing the night away on one of the most memorable evenings of Delia's life. This was truly a "die alive celebration." To live life to the fullest is to die alive. Learning to find the powerful lesson behind the most insidious life changes is the training ground for the concept of dying alive.

Carole was a wild and single mom just ending a long-term non-monogamous relationship when she realized that it was time to change her life pattern and engage in a deeper, more profound love of herself and her son and to find a new mate for life. She decided to perform a wedding to herself.

"The wedding to myself was one of the most powerful small death rituals that I have ever done. I wanted to go from wild woman to being monogamous and to having a solid father for my son. I wanted to be rooted and stable and able to experience a really deep love instead of a lot of very superficial loves. I wanted to trade experimentation for a profound relationship with a lifetime mate.

"I did a tea ceremony and read my new vows aloud to my closest friends so they would know how to help support and keep me on track in this new direction. Before the ceremony I dug a series of holes in which each guest would plant a flower representing new life. Into each hole I placed the words of letting go symbolizing my old ways and life patterns that were dying and no longer healthy for me. After the ceremony each guest planted her flower, which symbolized the simultaneous burial of the old and the marriage of the new. We all planted flowers in the garden, then tied wishes for the new life onto a tree outside of my door. I had a card printed that listed my vows, my needs, and my determination to find and marry my eternal mate. When I would meet someone that I thought was a definite possibility, I would give him this card. Many men thought it was very offensive. Way too brash. I didn't waste my time on them. Most of my creative energy was diverted to my search. It took me six months to find my mate and we have been together ever since."

Daphne designed a very personal ritual for her woman friends to mark her seventieth birthday. She recalls, "I sing in a small choir and one of the members wrote a special song for the occasion. To me it sounded like the voices of angels and set the tone for the evening. My friends shared their hopes for me in my aging and told stories of experiences we had shared over the years. My oldest friend from high school put together a memory book that included photos from different times in my life. I will treasure it always.

"People from all different phases of my life were there—45 women in all. Just looking around at those precious women who represented so many life transitions filled my heart.

"We had a ceremony where we each made an origami dove out of white rice paper and wrote on it a change we hoped to make in our lives. We hung the doves from dowels and had the best time making a mobile as we chanted 'fly away, fly away, little bird.'

"This celebration made me realize that I want to focus on those I love while I am alive and can give and receive joy. It is so rewarding to bring together the people I most care about. I am already planning my next party as I intend to feel totally partied before I die!"

~

KATHY

Kathy Barr, a professional writer and illustrator living in San Francisco, recently experienced a long period of time during which she felt her creative impulses were dying. One night as she lay in bed, she imagined that she was actually shooting her most loved books with a gun. She felt that if she shot them, the lines would be torn apart and the words would be released so they could return to her. Kathy pictured the books with a piece of glass in front of them so as the bullet hit, it shattered the surface first to get through to the words and pierce the heart of the writing. She carried this image in her mind for months.

One day, Kathy decided to act out her vision. She drove to a friend's house who lived in the country where she felt physically, personally, and artistically safe. She took with her the books that were most important to her: Thomas Mann's *Death in Venice* and *Magic Mountain*, D. H. Lawrence's *Women in Love*, and a couple of books by Samuel Beckett. At her friend's place, she set one of her books on a side hill away from the house and placed a piece of wire-imbedded glass in front of it. Using a .22 rifle, she aimed and fired again and again, the loud crack of the explosion echoing through the valley. Her friends watched to give her support. Kathy's ritual was experiential as well as visual, literal as well as symbolic. After shooting all of the books, Kathy felt a great satisfaction.

Afterwards, while soaking in a hot tub and remembering the experience, a long awaited line of poetry tumbled out of her. Something defnitely had shifted for her. She could write again.

~

SUSAN

By the time Susan discovered that she had breast cancer, it had spread into her lymph glands and moved to 'stage two.' She was told she would need a mastectomy.

It was terrifying to be facing death so suddenly and having to make the decision to cut off a piece of her body. She felt as though she didn't have time to process everything that was happening to her. She wanted to kick and scream and put the brakes on what felt like a runaway train. Susan had always been committed to alternative medicine, so it was very difficult for her to consider the medical model of chemotherapy and mastectomy.

Several members of her women's group had gone with Susan to her appointments as her treatment options were being discussed. From the beginning when she first learned about her lump, they had been involved. The group was extremely close and had been creating rituals together for years. It seemed natural to her friends to create a ritual for Susan, whom they loved and admired.

One of the members of the group described the ritual, "We gathered under weeping willow trees at the edge of a small private lake on a warm September afternoon and took off our blouses to bind us together in our womanhood. Sitting together on a beautiful blanket, we created a sacred circle space for Susan. We smudged our bodies with a sage smoke to help us let go of the ordinary world and step into the sacred. We laid Susan down on the blanket and very lovingly painted her body with grease paints and watercolors.

"Susan created a cast of her breast out of clay and took an impression of it. As she did this we chanted and told stories about the Amazon women who only had one breast so they could shoot their bows with ease.

"Although it was clear that Susan needed to have a mastectomy in order to save her life, it was through the ritual process that Susan finally was able to make peace with the sacrifice of her breast.

"One of the most beautiful images was seeing Susan with her long flowing hair and painted body paddling alone in a canoe out to the middle of the lake. She looked strong as she glided over the water. When she reached the center of the lake, she sat for a long time meditating on the act she was about to perform. She tossed beautiful fresh flowers onto the surface of the water. These spoke to her of beauty beyond society's notion of a beautiful body. When she felt ready, Susan let her "breast" slip into the beautiful green waters of the lake and it quickly sank out of sight.

"At the hospital the next day, her friends circled her bed just before she went into surgery and passed on to her their love and strength."

Susan believes that the ritual positively affected her attitude toward the whole experience and helped her to heal more quickly, both emotionally and physically. Within a couple hours after surgery, she was up having a lovely dinner with friends. The ritual itself was powerful medicine that worked energetically on so many levels.

Life is an ongoing test that can find you pushed to your limits again and again. You can break down at these points or choose to break through. You can step up to the threshold of the next phase and open that unknown door in your life or you can continue to control, regulate, and try to force the world to submit to your preconceived plan. Determined action will expand your concept of life, and the universe will open up and begin working with you. Practice and risk taking is necessary if you are to create a new blueprint for dying alive. The practice is to continually embrace your own personal creative fire. Out of this fire emerges the phoenix of new forms, new loves, and a more spirited way of being.

CHAPTER TWO

Temple Maintenance:
How Your Worldly Goods Strengthen
Your Spiritual Legacy

Temple maintenance has to do with caring for the spiritual side of life as well as the practical—things as simple as picking a fresh flower and placing it on your desk, or lighting the candle on your dinner table and taking some moments to acknowledge your blessings. When you are nurturing your temples of body, soul, and mind, you'll notice the quality of daily life begins to soar. When your temple is in a state of order, the small deaths that life regularly offers up will not be so overwhelming.

If you enjoy the feeling of spring house cleaning or putting your office in order, you know how good it can feel to make practical and spiritual estate decisions. Making sensible, responsible decisions will free you from the worry of leaving an entanglement of unsolved mysteries for those you love after you die. The internal peace is a bonus gift to yourself.

It is extremely liberating to live with your emotional bags packed. After years of procrastination I have finally put my house in order. Now that I am a grandmother, I decided to simplify my life and make arrangements for the people who will be dealing with my estate after I am gone.

I know how hard it can be to get your estate in order. It's so difficult that the majority of Americans don't even have a simple will. We really don't want to leave a mess behind us for others to untangle, but our rejection of death is so prevalent that we just don't seem to get around to doing the paperwork.

To sort out your legacy you must sort through your thoughts and feelings about the people as well as the things in your life. The first thing that you will be acknowledging on a practical level is that you *are* going to die. Of course, we all are, but it is still an emotionally demanding realization. For most of us, death is the event we are most afraid of. The big payoff to all this hard work is that you will get to live your life more fully. As with any psychic log jam that you free up, you will have a lot more creative energy. If you haven't begun the process, I urge you to begin now. People who have procrastinated too long end up full of regret when they find themselves near the end of their life and without the strength or focus to complete their estate plans.

Your Estate

Your estate includes much more than monetary assets. It is everything you own, including cars, real estate, jewelry, paintings, books, stocks, your business, your trophies, everything. Even if you don't own a home or have stocks and bonds, you still have an estate. Millionaire or pauper, everyone has an estate.

In addition to any money and property you have accumulated, you will also want to pass on your most important possessions to those you love. Those possessions imbued with your personal energy will be especially valued. Regardless of the size or type of your gifts, chances are they will have tremendous meaning and value to those you love.

In the 'Good Old Days'

Dividing possessions and property was simpler when firmly entrenched traditions dictated how people disposed of their worldly goods. Since before the Industrial Age, it was traditional to pass real property from one generation to the next, preferentially through the male line. In most European cultures the first-born son had preferred inheritance status, succeeding his father as head of the family and receiving the bulk of any land, livestock, wealth, etc. In Near Eastern countries he received a double portion of inheritance and was given the seat of honor amongst his brothers. Even here in the more egalitarian United States, the oldest son was normally the recipient of the majority of the family's assets. He took over the farm or the family business and was expected to take care of his mother and unmarried sisters.

Daughters, on the other hand, often received the family silverware, furniture, and other heirlooms. A younger brother might get a few tools, a wagon, and some books. Except in the wealthiest of families, inheritance was more about possessions and property than actual money.

While not particularly fair, this tradition of primogeniture was at least predictable. Sons who worked on the family farm or in the family business were also more likely to be educated; but daughters were not. Because women were expected to be wives and mothers and be taken care of by *their* husbands, it made sense to give the lion's share of the assets to the eldest son, who was often the most experienced and responsible sibling.

The last century saw most of the old traditions of the inheritance of property disappear. Thoughtful planning involves a creative balancing of emotional considerations and legal issues and ensures that your intentions are both clear and legally viable. It can be a challenge to create a workable estate plan, but it can also enrich your life to do so. It offers you the opportunity to leave a legacy of love, healing, and in some cases, forgiveness.

It's important to plan the distribution of your assets before death is imminent, so you aren't too exhausted or preoccupied to give it the proper attention. Death can happen unexpectedly, so it's important to fulfill the legal requirements now to ensure that your wishes will be carried out. The one thing worse than not making a will at all is making a poorly written will.

Conscious planning is more than just having good intentions. "Thinking you're giving money and actually giving money are two different things," warns CPA Reuben Weinzveg. "By all means, get professional help. Make sure your intentions do not run afoul of the tax code and estate laws."

An estate-planning attorney for nearly two decades, Rob Disharoon, agrees. "Deal with it," he says. "Many people say 'I don't have an estate. The Kennedys and Rockefellers have estates.' The word *estate* scares people away. Estate just means what you have." Even if all you have are a few photo albums, a high school ring, and a recliner chair, it's important to make your wishes known. If you don't have a plan to distribute your monetary assets and treasures, someone else will decide what happens to them for you. It might be a forgotten relative who doesn't know who your closest friends are or the name of your favorite charity. It might be a relative you don't even like who might cut out your fiancée or nonmarried spouse or make a terrible decision regarding your children. If you have no relatives, it will be the state that will decide. Without a will, for example, the state court determines who'll care for your children when you are gone.

Write a Will

Despite everything that goes wrong with not having a will, there is a lot of resistance to sitting down and writing one. On our list of priorities,

If you don't want to or can't afford to hire an attorney or CPA, Nolo.com has comprehensive resource materials to help you do it all yourself. The mission of Nolo.com is to help people "take the law into their own hands." They have been in business for 30 years and publish over 100 self-help legal products including books with forms and step-by-step instructions, books with form-rich floppies and CDs, and the popular *WillMaker* and *Living Trust Maker* programs. They provide an online legal encyclopedia for the most up-to-the-minute legal information available.

The computer program, *WillMaker*, has sold over 6,000,000 copies—more wills than any lawyer or law firm in history has ever written. Developed by a team of attorneys, it is updated periodically to reflect changes in the law and it contains an icon to alert users to situations that require the services of a professional.

In this top quality will-writing program you can also write and customize your living will, financial power of attorney, and final arrangement documents with confidence.

Since 70% of people don't have any will at all, *WillMaker* fills a very important niche. Many of us are reluctant to set up a will even though we know we should. There is a major difference between knowing we should do something and actually doing it. In an age when people are beginning to take a more active role in their healthcare and other aspects of their lives, *WillMaker* makes sense. And you don't even have to leave home to craft this extremely important document.

See the Resource section for more by Nolo.com

making a will seems way down near the bottom. Stop procrastinating! Putting important things off is unnecessarily stressful and can have dire consequences.

One day my friend Bronwyn expressed her concern about putting off making a will. "Our project this year is to do the living will and to take care of other legal matters. I'm terrified what the legal effect might be on our small child if something happens to us. I really want to get it taken care of but I keep putting it off. I live with a husband who doesn't deal with these things very well either. I have to keep nudging him as well as myself. I know from firsthand experience that if you don't take care of it, your children are going to have to do it. I had to do it for both my parents, and it was horrible. They left no directions, and nobody knew what to do or where anything was. It was totally unfair to us. My father had no will, and he was bankrupt. He left a lot of old debts that we had to take care of. It was like having to clean up a toxic waste dump."

Choose an Executor

An executor is the person who will be legally responsible for carrying out your wishes as set out in your will. The executor should be someone you trust, who preferably lives nearby. Some estates take years to settle, and travel could be a burden. Your executor should know you as well as your family and can even be a family member. Be sure to put the concerns of your heart first before the legal abilities of the executor because lawyers and accountants can be hired. Someone who knows and cares about you and your family is invaluable. Choose someone who is in good health, and it's a good idea to choose an alternate or successor executor in case your original choice can't fulfill his or her duties for any reason. If you have more than one child, you might choose to name all of your children so that no one child has the burden of the work involved and no child feels you didn't trust him or her enough with the responsibility. In some cases this choice brings children closer and in others it can be cumbersome and divisive. This is a delicate matter and deserves much thought and, hopefully, discussion with each child.

Remember to ask any potential executor in advance, making sure she or he understands what being an executor entails, and review your wishes with her often enough so she is kept up-to-date.

"Family members and good friends whom you would choose for your executor are not the same as estate planners, lawyers, or accountants," notes Bruce Dzieza, a financial planner based in Sebastopol, California. "Often people name their estate planner as their executor, which then legally excludes them from being advisors. Or they designate a bank, which is a very impersonal choice. The banker you have dealt with for the past decade might move on, and you are left with an institution, not a person you trust, administering your affairs. A good rule of thumb is to designate someone who represents your heart and let them hire expert advice if they need it.

"Be really clear with whomever you choose and give them guidance as to specific ways you would like the money used—for education, a first house, starting a business, travel, etc."

Parents and Their Children—Children and Their Parents

Just about everyone has something of value to leave their children. Even if it isn't important to you or something of significant monetary value, it can make a big difference to your children. The more clearly your wishes are expressed in writing, the less chance there will be for things to go awry. Most important, sit down and discuss plans if your children are old enough, and listen to their feedback. Make sure that any agreements or promises made are written down and included in your will.

"Many parents are reluctant to talk to children about their plans, if they have them," Rob Disharoon, estate planner, notes. "They don't want to worry them. They don't want their kids to think they're ill or contemplating suicide. However, discussing plans in advance can help clarify parents' wishes and in some cases, provide rationale for doing what they're doing. Often children don't want to admit their parents might die, and they discourage conversation or downright refuse to participate in any discussion about death. If your children are reluctant to discuss even the idea that you might die, write them a note assuring them you are just fine but for your own peace of mind you need to discuss your estate plans. Include an invitation to dinner or a walk in the park."

Bruce Dzieza knows that children also feel awkward bringing up estate questions with their parents. "When kids come to the office they confess they don't know where the safety deposit box keys are or anything else about their parents' affairs." I tell them, "When your parents are seventy or eighty years old, it's ok to go ask them where things are. It's a good way to start talking together. Many of the people I have suggested this to have come back and said it was a wonderful experience."

Most of our lives are very complex, so to make life easier for your heirs it's helpful to make a list of things they might have difficulty finding, such as the location of your safety deposit key and at which bank your box is located. It's common for people to put everything, such as a will and other important documents, in the box, forgetting banks are closed on weekends and their lawyer is not always available. Wherever you decide to keep this list make sure several people know its whereabouts. There are many details you might want to include. For example, if a lot of your important information is stored on your computer, be sure your executor knows your password. Include on your list the contact information of your insurance agent, spiritual advisor, emergency pet guardian, and all the details of your life. Be prepared—it will be a long list!

I recommend purchasing *Before I Go, You Should Know*, an end-of-life planning kit packaged in a see-though plastic button-tie pouch that can be stored in your freezer. This is handy for you when you remember important documents that should be included and handy to anyone who needs the information to care for you. Included is a state-specific Living Will and other advance directives, a 20-page booklet for you to write in, a checklist of other important documents, and a refrigerator magnet that informs people that matters of life and death are inside. I keep one in my freezer and take one with me when I go on a trip. Some people keep one in their glove compartment of their car. This kit is available from your local Funeral Consumers Alliance. See Resources.

Bequesting Guidelines

Here are some guidelines to consider when estate planning with children in mind:

∾ Get Professional Help: Don't even attempt to set up your own trusts or write your own will without professional guidance or review. Laws change constantly, and a minor oversight in wording can lead to an unwelcome outcome. Keep it up to date as your family's resources and needs change. A good way to keep your will up to date is to review it every year at tax time.

∾ Be Clear About Your Wishes: Communicate your wishes and the reasons for them, especially if you plan to treat children or grandchildren unequally. *How you divide up your assets is your prerogative.*

However, it can be very distressing to those left behind not to have an understanding of your wishes explained either in the paperwork or verbally. It's best to do both. Writing down the reasons is important, because memories are imperfect. Provide a rationale so your heirs will understand why you did what you did and will not spend the rest of their lives torturing themselves with unanswered questions.

When my friend Lonny died at the age of eighty-two, she left her son and daughter the bulk of her estate. Her son, although attentive and loving, lived all of his adult life 3,000 miles from his parents. Lonny's daughter lived half an hour from her parents, called them daily, helped out whenever needed anything, and was actively involved in their lives. When Lonny's assets were divided, everything was equal except for a bank account held in trust for her son, with $25,000 in it. There was no such account in her daughter's name.

Did Lonny assume her daughter's husband would take care of her, and her son, therefore, should get the extra money? Or was it just an oversight? Had she planned to open an account for her daughter, too, but never got around to it? Sadly, this became a painful, nagging question for Lonny's daughter. She will never know the truth and the question gnaws at her. She even asked her widowed father about it, but all he can say is, "Your mother was always fair. Everything was 50–50. I don't understand it either." In the daughter's mind her memory of her mother and her relationship with her brother are forever tainted.

Estate planning attorneys tell me that this type of situation is all too common. Yet unanswered questions, hurt feelings, and lingering doubts are all avoidable. If only Lonny had put an explanation of the discrepancy in her will or told her daughter about it before she died, the issue would not have been so difficult. Parents have every right to dispose of their assets in whatever ways feel right and appropriate, but it is unfair and hurtful not to provide an explanation if there is any inequity.

A funeral director told me about an eccentric millionaire he knew who made a video years before he died, in which he explained to his children why he was giving all his money to his favorite charity instead of to them. His hopeful heirs were shocked and angry when the attorney shut off the VCR, but at least they understood why their father had made this choice. The self-made millionaire loved his children and firmly believed that unearned wealth created more problems than it solved. Although he had always been open about his feelings, his children hadn't really grasped the strength of his belief. Like most of us, they had heard what they wanted to hear. Of course, they weren't happy about not getting the inheritance they had expected, but they at least understood it and could move on with their grief and disappointment.

If the family home is the biggest asset and the children have different economic considerations, it's especially important to be clear. Don't let your nostalgic feelings or theirs muddy the waters. It's difficult to anticipate if one of the children might want to live in the house and another needs the money and forces a sale, for example. Do whatever it takes to keep things clear and as uncomplicated as possible. Don't leave it to your children to untangle a big mess after you are gone.

↬ Loans: Loans from parents to children are another issue requiring sensitive handling. If there have been loans made to one sibling and not to another, put a note in your will to offset the inheritance.

I once knew a brother and a sister who were left equal amounts of money by their parents, but the brother had borrowed thousands of dollars over the years from his parents and had never repaid any of it. The sister, although better off financially, felt cheated because her inheritance was considerably less than it might have been since a large percentage of the parents' estate had been "drained" over the years.

Although the sister didn't need the money, she still wanted what was rightfully hers, and more importantly, she needed to be acknowledged by her parents. For her, "It's not about the money, it's about the principle." The brother, in a much less secure financial position than his sister, refused to repay the estate and felt justified in not doing so. His argument: "My sister has and can afford everything she wants. She never has to work a day in her life. She married big money and lives like a princess. I wasn't as lucky. She doesn't need the money, and I do. How greedy can she get?" The brother didn't understand that his sister's emotional needs (which must be recognized equally) were being expressed through the metaphor of money.

∾ Guardianship: When our children are young and vulnerable we need to protect them, provide for them, and shelter them. One of the biggest challenges can be to choose a legal guardian for them in case both parents should die. Sometimes the closest relative may not be the best choice. Factors such as the guardian's age, lifestyle, relationship to your children, and willingness to parent must be considered. It is critical to have an open discussion with the intended guardian to make sure they would be willing to care for your children in the event of a tragedy. It's important to review your wishes regularly with the intended guardians, as situations are bound to change.

For example, when I discussed guardianship with Sara and Geoff, who have three children age nine, seven, and four, it became clear that even though they had a will, it needed to be changed. Sara has diabetes and lives with the constant worry that she might die before her children are grown and that her husband would be unable to care for them on his own. The relatives they had originally designated as guardians eight years earlier now have five children of their own, one of whom is disabled. Geoff's brother and his wife were delighted with the honor of guardianship of one child eight years ago, before they had any children of their own, but at this point in their lives they would be totally overwhelmed with the addition of three children to their family. In fact, when Geoff and Sara reminded them of the situation, they had totally forgotten they had ever agreed to act as guardians.

In some situations, more than one guardian, or sets of guardians, may make good sense. Some friends of mine struggled over whom to name as guardians when they were preparing their wills after the birth of their second child. They had a large extended family, but they couldn't decide which relatives would be the best guardians—especially since children's needs differ at various ages. They worked out a creative solution by naming two different sets of guardians in their will. They felt one couple would be better at meeting the needs of the children when they were small, and another set of guardians were named in the event the parents died when the children were adolescents or older, as this couple was more educationally oriented and this mattered a great deal to the parents.

Personal Communications

A spiritual legacy is more than how people remember you after you are gone. It is honoring your deepest connections, what you stood for, believed in, worked to accomplish, your values, life lessons, and gifts to humanity.

∾ Make a videotape of a day in your life or take your favorite still photos and have a camera shop turn them into a video. It can be as simple or as elaborate or as long or short as you want. Be sure to include important events like birthdays and anniversaries, creating a living scrapbook for your loved ones.

∾ Walk through your home with a friend and have them video you as you point out favorite treasures, naming who you would like to receive each one. This tape can be left with your will.

∾ Make a special remembrance book. Remember the baby books you had as a child? Perhaps you made one for your own children. This is a life book—your life. Paint in it. Glue in photos. Write down treasured conversations or events. Pass on your wisdom. Include anything that you would like people you care about to have. If you need several copies, have favorite pages color Xeroxed and spiral bound at a print shop.

∾ Write an ethical will. An ethical will is a love letter to your family and is as unique as the person writing it. An ethical will is an ancient legacy that is once more becoming popular. It typically includes your spiritual values, life's lessons, blessings for future generations, and forgiving or asking for forgiveness from others. For more information visit www.ethicalwills.com.

∾ Record an audiotape. It's such an emotionally powerful gift to be able to hear a voice again whenever you want. Include music if you play or sing your favorite songs or read a poem you find inspiring.

∾ Write individual letters to your children, spouse, or anyone who holds an important place in your heart.

Creative Giving

∽ Prepare a list of what items you want to go to whom. You may wish to ask your children, partners, lovers, and friends what items are significant to them. There may be some surprises!

∽ Suggest to your children in your will that if they have a conflict in dividing up your personal property they might take turns by picking straws or rolling dice. If this doesn't work, they could appoint an objective, third-party arbitrator to be there to keep the peace. It is important to know your children's choices, and helpful to gather them together to make these choices before you die.

Farley Wheelwright, a Unitarian Universalist minister and his wife Virginia gathered their children together one Christmas to deal with the division of their possessions. "We got all four children together, gave them each a pad and pen, and turned them loose in our Boston home, which is filled with our lifetime collection of antiques and art treasures, to make their choices. We were hoping that they would want just a few things, because we have a good art collection that we could sell and use for our retirement. They wanted everything! They wanted the rugs, they wanted the china, they wanted the paintings, they wanted it all. When the children came together and compared their lists, there were, inevitably, conflicts. So, we all talked about it together and made compromises. As a group, we decided who was going to get what right then and there with us, and Virginia and I wrote it all down.

"At this time in our lives it feels good to be free of all that stuff. Stuff is a burden. Our feeling is that by doing it this way it's going to be a lot more orderly. What a nightmare if we died and they all came to Boston and had to figure it all out on the spot."

∾ Give away personal possessions you no longer want or need while you're alive to see your children enjoy the fruits of your labor. If you are really concerned that division of your estate will leave bad feelings among siblings, or if you don't feel particularly creative, you might want to consider the advice of the bumper sticker "We are spending our children's inheritance."

∾ If you choose to have any of your children be the executor of your estate, consider having all the siblings be executors or trustees, or at least two if there are multiple siblings. Bring all your capable adult children into the process. Some estate settlements can take a few years, so when only one child is named executor, others often end up feeling left out and the burden of the estate and probate work is unfairly heaped upon the executor. This can bring up feelings of suspicion, resentment, and the potential for disputes.

Eddie's story is a good example of how a parent can set the stage for discord without meaning to. Without thinking it through, he had chosen only one of his sons to be the executor of his estate. By designating the investment banker son as executor, he thought he was doing everyone a favor. Without even discussing it with him, Eddie made the assumption that his other son, a sculptor, would feel burdened with the job. Both of Eddie's sons resented each other and the roles they had grown up fulfilling within the family. The banker resented the fact that his brother got to be creative and lived what he considered a rather irresponsible life style. The sculptor, on the other hand, resented the fact that because his brother had a more conventional life and career, he was considered more successful.

In making his banker son the sole executor, Eddie would only be reinforcing both brothers' roles and resentments. When updating his will, his estate-planning attorney suggested that it might be a more compassionate choice to make his sons co-executors. By doing so, he would send a clear message that he valued his sons equally and could demonstrate his trust and respect for them both. Eddie also realized that this would provide them with the opportunity to appreciate each other's way of life by working together.

~ Think carefully about the legacy that you want to leave. If there are strained relations in your family, sensitive estate planning can provide an opportunity to help heal old wounds and perhaps even bring your family closer together.

I love this story of a widow whose family had been in the dairy business for generations who inherited a dairy worth several million dollars. She had three children, who hadn't spoken to each other for years. She named each of them in her will as executors for the estate with the provision that they have a facilitator to help them. Before she died, she gathered her children together and explained what she was doing and why. She let them know that she understood that by setting up her estate this way she would be virtually forcing them to resolve their conflicts and work together, and that she hoped they could meet the challenge. They would have to get along and reach consensus or they would never get a dime. After two years of working with the facilitator to settle the estate, and with the estate as a motivator, they became a family again. In her death, their mother had reunited them, leaving a legacy of love that was truly priceless.

Set aside a day or evening to appreciate your treasures. You might want to invite a good friend, unplug the phone, and look at the possessions you have collected over the years with an eye to passing them on. Some you probably no longer notice, others make up the day to day beauty of your life. Make three piles.

~ Pile one is the 'spring cleaning no longer need pile'—these are passed on to the Salvation Army, Good Will, or local hospice thrift shop.

∾ Pile two is to give away now so you can share in the enjoyment while you are alive. That vase your sister covets, your mother's china that your sister-in law has always wanted, the antique car sitting in your garage that Fred gets misty-eyed over, the first edition of *Raggedy Andy* your son could now read to his son.

∾ Pile three is the things you are not yet ready to part with. Take time to savor each of them, then write down who might enjoy particular items, and include the list in your remembrance book or put it with your will. Even better, photograph them and write the recipients name, phone number, and address on the back of the photo and place it in your remembrance book.

Each of us will leave a legacy when we die. How we plan for the distribution of our spiritual and material assets helps determine the kind of legacy we leave. Inheritance is as old as human civilization. The passing on of the fruits of our life's work, personal items we've lived with and loved, and other heirlooms are only part of our legacy. The way we handle the division of our material goods and money sends an important farewell message to family and friends, a message that communicates our values as well as the respect and love we shared during our lifetime—a message that becomes a large part of the legacy we leave.

Organ, tissue, and body donation

Each day 60 people receive an organ transplant but another 16 on the waiting list die. I urge you, if possible, to consider a generous gift to the living with an organ donation. All major religions approve of organ and body donations for transplants, teaching, and research purposes.

The Partnership for Organ Donation (transweb.org/partnership) is an independent nonprofit that is closing the gap between the number of transplants possible and those that actually occur. Their Web site provides valuable information.

Some medical schools require donor registration before death, while others accept bequests from the next-of-kin with no prior arrangement. Many people designate a medical school, but if they don't or if this is a bequest from the survivors, the National Anatomical Service (NAS) 1-800-727-0700 has 24-hour service and can link you with schools with the greatest need.

The American Medical Association has a comprehensive Web site that can help answer questions you may have about organ and tissue donations. They also have links to improve organ donation awareness by using the Internet.

CHAPTER THREE

Handcrafting Potent Ceremonies for Death

Death rituals are universal, time-honored traditions rooted in good psychology. A meaningful death ritual can reinforce your humanity and recharge you during a traumatic time. As you begin to honor your creativity and make a better quality of life for yourself, being mindful of spiritual experiences pertaining to death becomes especially important.

The purpose of a funeral or memorial service is to honor a life and give comfort to the living, and it is too important to leave to chance or to strangers. Generic rituals are usually emotionally draining and do not allow you to access your deepest feelings. A truly personalized death ritual, however, can provide the real comfort needed to pave the way for healing to occur. Contemplating and even planning death rituals before you are in a crisis situation helps you to be better prepared when someone dies.

Sukie Miller, Ph.D., is the author of *After Death*, a cross-cultural study of afterdeath rituals and beliefs. She describes ritual this way: "Ritual is the doorway between one reality to another. Ritual is the container.

Either there are other dimensions of reality or there are not. If there are, then rituals have to be the bridge between both of these dimensions. Ritual has three parts: The first is for the sake of the person who is going to die, so that he will have some sense of what will happen after he dies, which is a lovely thing. The second part is for the people who are left behind, so that they have community and are not alone in their grieving. And the third part is for the person who is dead.

"We are a materialistic culture, and we have to learn from other cultures, we have to consider what's possible. We are not a culture of ritual. We live with death and we think we are crazy. Other cultures live with death and have a ritual to contain this. They have a way to cope with it. They say, 'Okay after twenty-one days you do this.' 'After seven years you do that.'

"There are two ways to look at the ritual. One is that it is soothing and comforting and allows one to get some control over the future. The other is how you look at time. If you go to other countries the purpose of these death rituals is not for the living. It is for the dead. In our culture we have a very narcissistic way of looking at ritual—that it's about us and helping us feel better. But what about the person who died?

"Americans have a very limited understanding of time. You go outside of our culture and time does not have a beginning, middle, and end. Time is ever onward. Some systems wait a thousand years before they come back. Other systems go on space ships to another world. Other systems go to a world where everything we have here is there.

"It's my concern and my belief that it's very important that we know what we believe about our afterdeath. Even if you believe that nothing happens and you become a molecule or not even that, that's still an afterdeath belief. Everybody has a belief. It's there. It's lurking. It's bubbling. What's important is to find out what it is and to engage it. To plan around it and to support it. The content is secondary.

"The overall purpose of my work is to begin a dialogue about afterdeath in a personal way. To give us a language. We do not have a language to talk about the afterdeath. I'm going to be lifted in the arms of Jesus. Okay, but what is this going to feel like. Is it going to be drafty? Will you have wings? How will he hold you if you have wings? What will Jesus feel like? These are things we need to talk about. This is not verboten. Who knows? Nobody knows. So let's talk."

Ceremony connects us with each other. In connecting with each other we find ourselves. Baby boomers have been remaking their own wedding ceremonies and birth rituals for several decades. It is natural that we now create meaningful alternatives to the traditional ceremonies accompanying death.

Ritual can play an important role in both honoring the dead and helping the survivors move on to the next phase of their lives. It helps heal the psyche by creating a way for the living to come to terms with loss and grief, both individually and as a community. A powerful ceremony creates a way of making spiritual feelings visible and allows friends to help each other grieve.

Maille Arnold is a landscape consultant, teacher, and dedicated organic gardener very much attuned with nature's rhythms. One afternoon in her magnificent garden she shared with me this story of the last ritual she shared with her mother:

"The last ten years of my mother's life were difficult," Maille recalled. "She had always been athletic and outdoorsy, but her heart rhythm was damaged and so she slowly became more and more tired and less and less able to swim and run and walk and do all the things that had always been important to her. Mother believed that her spirit continued in her children and in her memories. She wanted to be cremated and have her ashes scattered.

"The one special place in her life that she would return to again and again is our property on the northeast shore right on the beach. She enjoyed swimming at our place there so much. She loved the very clear windless Kula winter weather when you can see all the way up the mountains and way out to sea when the air and the ocean are still. It was her favorite time and her continual place of refuge all her life, so we decided that each child and my stepfather would distribute her ashes there as we chose.

"As she was dying, one of the things that I did was take her on the walk that I was going to take with her ashes while she could still hear me. I reminisced with her about the places where I was going to leave a little bit of her and shared the memories that I had in this little portion of the property or this part of the beach. We visited the place where we used to play paddle tennis and we shared the little stories over my lifetime of things mother and I had done together. It was the most magical walk to do with her while she was still alive and then for her to know that I would visit with her anytime I went by those places. Then, of course, I did the walk later and every time I'm there I do it again.

"During Mom's last weeks we washed and brushed and curled her hair. We put cream on her hands, her feet, her face. We painted her fingernails and toenails. We did all the things that she loved. She had the most gorgeous view of the Iao Valley from her hospital bed, and every night before we left we would turn her head on the pillow so she could look up the valley. She had this doll that her best friend had brought her, and we would show it to her because she couldn't look down anymore and then we would put the doll in her arms and then off we'd go every night. I love what Jennifer Stone says, "Go easy and if you can't go easy, go easy as you can." That's what we were doing—we were going as easy as we could and trying to help Mom to go as easy as she could."

Ceremonies

It seems strange that in our modern culture we spend vast amounts of time and money to personally orchestrate weddings, sweet sixteen parties, anniversary celebrations, Bar and Bat Mitzvahs, and other important rights of passage. Yet, when it comes to death, we seem at a loss and typically turn over all arrangements to a death professional.

Though no longer pioneers, Americans are still a transient society. We move frequently, sometimes never putting down roots in a community. In many cases, we have no strong spiritual affiliation, and so the members of the funeral industry have assumed the role of designated grief counselors in addition to handling all of the funeral arrangements for ourselves and those we love. These death professionals don't know us or our community ties and are increasingly part of a giant chain of funeral parlors with all that implies.

Most of us have attended inappropriate funeral ceremonies, impersonal, dismal affairs that had little to do with whatever made the deceased person special. Death rituals, for the most part, have evolved into stagnant generic renditions—efficient, but artificial and lacking in meaning. Instead of being comforted, the mourners are left feeling adrift, isolated and uncared for.

Interestingly, when a violent and senseless community tragedy occurs, people instinctively know what to do. Each person reacts naturally and does what feels right for herself. They may gather where the death occurred or designate a site and come together, each grieving in his or her own way. They bring flowers and poems, stories, songs, they build shrines, and spontaneously pay tribute to the dead. There is no leader, no "right" way, the ritual flows naturally from each heart. The outpouring of heartfelt emotion in the community of Columbine, Colorado, is a perfect example of spontaneous grieving and remembrance.

Death, on a more personal level, however, leaves us confused and feeling adrift. We may find ourselves caught between what we feel we should do and the dictates of tradition. It would be so much easier and reassuring if we could trust ourselves to know what to do, if we could find solace in traditions that hold real meaning for us instead of having to create a new context at a time when we are emotionally drained.

I believe we are confused because few of us have had personal, family, or community training when it comes to dealing with death, nor do we celebrate any yearly honoring rituals of the dead. We think that death professionals must know what to do, so we turn helplessly to them. Our rituals and ceremonies around death have become diluted, commercialized, and are often devoid of the soulful connection we need, crave, and deserve.

Today death has been taken out of our homes and moved into the funeral homes. The death industry has become a cumbersome, self-protective, and sanitized bureaucracy. This is the result of a gradual change in our society as we have distanced ourselves from real life and death experiences.

The only people who feel totally confident about dealing with the dead are in the funeral business. The very existence of the funeral industry has created a void in our human experience, which has spilled over into memorials and rituals for the dead and dying as well. Instead of directing and using the services provided by death professionals, we have become intimidated and uninformed consumers. Instead of participating in an informed partnership, we automatically hand over the entire process to these professionals. The attitude of 'let's just get through this on a functional level, and then we'll have time to feel it later,' often prevails.

In *Harpers Magazine* (July, 1999) George Michelsen Foy wrote a poignant story entitled, *Burning Oliver, the Brief Life and Private Burial of an Infant Son.* Foy states, "I have always and instinctively distrusted morticians and other professional sympathizers. It strikes me as logical that a bulkhead of hypocrisy must be built into their solicitude, if only to protect themselves emotionally from the chronic erosion of loss. I see it as anathema that the final send-off of people whose stories you care about should be placed in the hands of those who must manufacture the emotions that connect them to the dead."

Anne Stine has led wilderness quests for eleven years and understands the value that ritual plays in marking a change and helping you move into the next phase of your life. Anne is an excellent leader and explains that what makes a ritual meaningful is that it be authentic to you:

"You can, of course, create rituals for yourself," she says. "There is no difference in ritual between the inside and outside if it's meaningful. The authority for ritual comes from you. It's not just the church or the spiritual leader or the shaman that can do it. We all can do it. Whatever comes to you is okay. It's okay no matter how crazy it sounds, no matter what you want to do. If it is meaningful to you it's yours and it's good. All ritual that has ever been created has come through an individual's own inner life and relationship to the earth.

"On the wilderness quests there is a whole part of the preparation that's called 'self-generated ceremony.' The quest participants get a lot of encouragement, permission, and guidance to just do whatever comes. A ceremony is not only the lighting of a candle or the burning of smudge or the making of fire or whatever we might associate more specifically with ceremony. It can be the brushing of teeth. It can be the changing of clothes. Sleep. A ceremony is a meaningful activity that's right for you in the moment. It heals the separation between the sacred and the profane because you are following what's inside.

"When I guide people in ways of ceremony I always ask them if it promotes self-love, if it awakens your heart in some way to yourself. If it scares you or it doesn't warm your heart, or if it doesn't appeal to you, then don't go towards it. You have to know the difference. A lot of people don't know the difference between what warms their hearts and makes them feel comforted and what doesn't. I want to be very careful not to tell people what to do. I want it to come from inside, then it's really going to be theirs.

"To get the wheels going look around you and see what you would like to undertake that would awaken your heart. If you like making fires then just sit and watch the fire and see what comes up in you. You could put something in that fire and you could have it represent something that you are ready to let go of. Or in the case of somebody who's feeling very lonely and needs comfort they need to find a way that will connect them with that feeling of comfort. Maybe that's going to be an object that's inherited from a beloved person or a picture of that person that they can put up in front of them. If it's a husband that's been gone and they've been married a long time, they might look at the picture and talk to the husband and ask them to speak back to them so they can be comforted. Or they can light a candle and put his picture on the altar and start talking to him or just sit down and pray. Prayer is a fabulous thing and almost everybody knows how to do that. Go inside and just let yourself get down on your knees and ask for what you want."

Death challenges us to be in the present more than any life experience other than birth. If you aren't prepared to release those deep feeling when death occurs, where do they go? Or where do they stay? Rituals that lack potency and power can drain you of your vitality and in some cases cause scars that last throughout your life, curtail grieving, and cause anger and confusion.

Jill vividly remembers her smiling parents at the front door giving her and her brother hugs and goodnight kisses on the night her father died. "There was great excitement in the air as my father and mother were going to a fabulous dinner being given to honor my father's business success and his acceptance into a prestigious professional organization. My parents looked gorgeous, father in a silk suit, mother in a long evening gown. They were very flirtatious with each other and so in love. The next thing I knew I was awakened in the morning by my mother and told that there has been an accident and my father was dead."

Even though her father died thirty years ago, Jill was still teary-eyed as she recalled the funeral: "The funeral was in Minnesota where my father grew up. He was buried in the family plot. From my child's vision, it was the darkness of it all that frightened me the most. The mirrors in my grandmother's Jewish home were covered with black cloth. Everyone was wearing black. A group of elderly men gathered in a circle, rocking and reciting the Kaddish. The people who came by the house spoke in hushed tones, looked sadly at me but did not speak to me. My grandmother was crying hysterically and moaning. The rain pattered on the windows. It was as if the whole world were crying.

"We drove through the rain to the funeral. My mother sat on one side of me and my grandmother sat on the other. My grandmother was crying and wailing. My mother did not want to cry. I tried to be strong for her. I felt if I cried it would make it harder for her to be strong. I shoved all my tears and grief down deep inside.

"My father's funeral was very formal and filled with strangers. People gave me sympathetic looks but kept their distance. Prayers were recited and we all repeated lines together. At the gravesite a rabbi, who did not know my father, spoke about him, saying he was a good husband, devoted father . . . words that could have been said about anyone. None of it was about my full-of-life, charismatic, teasing, brilliant father. We tossed handfuls of dirt over the casket, and then my father was gone.

"I held back my tears and grief without quite knowing why for years. I was twelve when my father died. I know now I felt very alone at a time when I needed friends and a sense of community that understood how great my loss was. I needed to hear stories about my father, what he had meant to everyone who knew him. He had lived a very full life. Everything about my father's funeral was impersonal and alienating, which prevented me from coming to terms with my grief for many years."

My friend Bronwyn remembers her mother's funeral as a nightmare: "My mother died when I was eighteen. She had a very tragic life. My parents divorced when I was about twelve, and she had been diagnosed as a 'paranoid schizophrenic.' She became more and more depressed. In the mental hospital she was diagnosed with breast cancer, and I think she just decided she didn't want to live. My mother had lived in a shoebox all her life and the box was getting smaller and so she pretty much died alone.

"When I heard she was dying I raced to the hospital. She was still awake and I remember saying to her 'I love you, Mom.' She couldn't talk but she squeezed my hand. Her fingers were cold and she was kind of green and she had a tube up her nose. I told her, 'You'll be better in the morning,' and she winced. I walked out of the room and about a half an hour later my father came in and said 'Come say good-bye to your mother.' It all felt very strange to me, almost like walking in a dream.

"Her funeral ceremony was absolutely horrible. My father, who had not had anything to do with my mother for some time, directed it. He chose to have her embalmed and placed in an open casket. I was so young and I had no idea of what to do. We sat in this tiny chapel with a few people who remembered my mother. The smell of formaldehyde throughout the chapel mixed with the smell of flowers was awful.

"Of course, the minister didn't know anything about my mother. He made what had to be a short, rehearsed, pat statement that had nothing to do with her, or us, or anything. At the end people filed past her casket. I remember getting up but I couldn't look at her. My sisters said she looked beautiful except there was a frown on her face. The whole thing was traumatic. It couldn't have been uglier or more pathetic or less like I would have liked to have remembered my mother.

"Afterwards my mother was cremated. We didn't have much money at the time, so her remains were put in the very highest level of the mausoleum so we couldn't even see where she was. I never went back. Everything was wrong about her death—dying in a hospital, the suddenness of it, the embalming, the funeral, the frown on her face. I have tried to distance myself from it, tried to forget it, but of course I can't."

These two stories are representative of hundreds of similar stories I've heard. We have been taught to be polite, to use the right fork, and all of the things that this culture feels are important to function in society, yet, there are no lessons in how to participate in the ritual and passage of death.

Barbara Peterson, an intensive care nurse for twenty-five years deals with people's feelings of helplessness on a daily basis. "There are no guidelines for what to do when someone dies," she states. "I wish that we could have a way to deal with death that would become just a natural part of our lives. But it's just not the way it is. There are phone calls and arrangements to make. When someone dies the closest family members and friends are in an altered state. At the same time they are usually in a strange, somewhat surreal hospital environment and don't know the rules. What is proper? What is improper? There is so much to be done, and done quickly."

Barbara wishes that more people could die at home so they might be surrounded by friends and family, rather than a bleak, sterilized hospital surrounding. The nurses who work in intensive care can and do make a difference. They try to provide warmth and understanding to families as death approaches.

"When there is no time to help survivors, they usually go out to sit in the lobby and pick up a phone book and look up mortuaries nearby. Most people don't know where to begin because they haven't thought about it. They haven't prepared for it. There is no preparation for handling death beyond the dying."

Fortunately there is a strong and growing movement of people who understand the importance of reclaiming death rituals, who are creating personalized good-byes for themselves and loved ones. These people can be an inspiration to us all.

Ritual helps you go into and unlock certain places that bring transformation, sometimes even without conscious understanding. When rituals are crafted with meaning, they can confer the occasion with magic.

My aunt was dying, and we put rose petals on her hands and on her arms. She'd been in a coma for weeks and we couldn't believe that she was still alive. There was no food going to her, only liquids and the morphine drip. We were doing comfort care.

Roses were in bloom so her room was full of them, which was lovely. We rolled the petals between our fingers to get the juice out of them and rubbed it into the skin of her hands and feet.

At this point her skin was cold; her hands and feet were getting very gray. It looked like the life was going out of them. Her daughter and I moved slowly, working the petals gently into her skin.

It was really beautiful and it smelled so good and the softness of the petals was so wonderful. There we were, touching her and caring for her and as we stood back it looked really lovely, like she was being decorated in a way that she deserved. This ritual seemed especially important in the environment of a sterile hospital.

Paula

When the spiritual is tapped into, the transition is brought into focus and can be understood on many levels.

We live in a culture full of words and intellectualizations. The talking self is always talking. Ritual goes deeper and connects into the mystery of life. The processing of death is very difficult when dealt with intellectually, as it brings up things that the mind ponders but cannot grasp.

For more than ten years Jill Goffstein has led and participated in rituals of all kinds. "When the death of a loved one occurs it affects us in a profound way. We have a deep need to participate in honoring this person, to tell why this life was meaningful and well lived, and to grieve together with family and friends.

"The first crucial days following a death set the tone for the healing process. What we do has an impact that can reverberate for years to come. If we are able to truly honor and commemorate this passing of a life in a meaningful and honest way within a setting that allows us to grieve deeply and openly with others, then we can lay to rest this first step of the grieving period and begin the process of putting our lives back together.

"A more personalized ritual can be a powerful vehicle for honoring the life of a loved one. Rituals are especially effective because they surpass words and reach beyond ordinary reality. They deepen our experience by connecting us with the greater mysteries of life and death. Ritual can help us move through the experience of loss and grief by giving us the opportunity to invoke Spirit and bring closure by grieving with those who share our loss.

"The time spent planning the ritual is a very important step in the process of grieving and healing during these first few days after a loved one has died. The planning process provides a crucial, positive focus, giving us cause to reminisce about the life that has ended; the impact this one human being has had on others' lives, the stories told about this person, and the shared memories and values. By reviewing and reflecting upon his or her life, we can more fully accept the reality of the loss and facilitate the beginning of the grieving process."

It is difficult to think clearly and invent appropriate rituals when someone has died if you haven't been adequately prepared. For more information, refer to "Steps to Creating a Memorial Ritual" in the Appendix.

We don't have to feel alienated from thinking about our own death or the death of someone we love. We don't have to endure the discomfort and absurdity of memorial services that don't do justice to the dead person's true spirit, services that are a distortion rather than a true reflection. Creating personalized, "hands-on" rituals is a choice that is ours to make, one that can provide comfort for all involved. In the next three chapters we will share many different kinds of rituals to light the fires of transformation around death.

CHAPTER FOUR

The Last Dance —
Creating Meaningful Rituals
for Others

Do not stand at my grave and weep.

I am not there.

I do not sleep.

I am a thousand winds that blow.

I am the diamond glints on snow.

I am the sunlight on ripened grain.

I am the gentle autumn rain.

When you awaken in the morning's hush

I am the swift uplifting rush of quiet birds

in circling flight.

I am the soft star that shines at night.

Do not stand at my grave and cry.

I am not there.

I did not die.

Native American Prayer

A good death ritual honors the deceased in a meaningful way and can be extremely powerful and healing for the survivors. A good death ritual creates a sacred space that encourages you to reach out and connect with other family members and friends at a time when you, and they, most need support. As you continue to grieve in the months and years to come, you can find comfort knowing you gave the deceased the best and most appropriate tribute possible.

A personalized death ceremony not only pays tribute to the dead, it also facilitates the healing process for the living. You have many options about how much or how little you want to orchestrate and participate in the ceremony. From the people I have talked with as well as from personal experience, I feel the more involved you are in the ceremony the less apt you are to feel helpless. You might choose to conduct the entire ceremony yourself or turn for guidance to a minister, rabbi, priest, or close friend. There is no one right way, and there are many more ways than the traditional.

It takes a lot of thought and sensitivity to handcraft a funeral, and you may think you won't be much help at such an emotional time. But when someone dear to us dies, nature envelops us in an altered state similar to shock so that we can get through the days ahead. It is a space similar to the space that occurs during birth where everything else seems to recede into the background. It is incredibly healing to focus on honoring the deceased in an authentic way instead of worrying about what is 'proper' and giving over the process to a 'professional.' Remember, there is no law preventing you from taking charge, only, perhaps, inexperience. This chapter will provide you with many models to help you create your own very personal rituals and help you think through how to honor the deceased, either by adapting rituals that you grew up with or by inventing new ones that are a creative expression of your love.

Here in the United States there are so many influences and practices available from our melting pot of many cultures—which may be the reason few traditional rituals are very complete or empowering. Because everyone is trying to fit in, the result is many rituals either have been done away with completely or diluted into pale reflections of the original ceremonies.

I urge you to consider looking after at least some aspects of the memorial or funeral of close friends and relatives yourself because so many people no longer have a religious affiliation and therefore have no person who really knows them trained to help create an appropriate tribute. Of course, religious leaders and death professionals may still play an important role at this difficult time; however, it is not required that you give over the process to clergy or funeral directors.

There may, of course, be good reasons why turning over a memorial or funeral service to someone else is appropriate. You may be too far away, or other family members may be attached to a traditional ceremony, for example. It's important to recognize that each person's passing will be different and each person's ritual will need to be different. You may have been attracted to this book because you have experienced a funeral of a relative or friend that did not feel quite right or did not say anything personal about this special person's life. I hope you will consider your options and keep your heart open as you read the following stories.

∼

MARK

Mark was a film producer who was loved by many and who lived a big, energetic life. When people heard of his death, they called from all over the country, wanting to be a part of his memorial ceremony. They recited poems they had written about him, sang songs that described his spirit, played his favorite classical music, and read letters they had received from him. His immediate family spent a week prior to the gathering putting together a truly extraordinary slide show of pictures of his life accompanied by music. This labor of love brought Mark to life one last time. The collective memoriam had a deeply moving affect on everyone. When this incredible evening was over, Mark's brother spoke for everyone when he said, "Ah, we have grieved well."

∼

JEFF

When Jill lost her 33-year-old brother, Jeff, she and her mother did not want a repeat performance of the cold, impersonal funeral that her father had been given. They found a rabbi who was willing to help them create a ritual that was relevant to Jeff's life. Because Jeff created collages in the style of the German artist, Kurt Schwitter, incorporating old yellowed train tickets, postage stamps, pieces of rusty metal, and weathered wood to create works of art, they decided to design Jeff's memorial as a collage of his life. Friends and family sat in a circle and described their relationships with Jeff. Everyone shared a story about him: How he had inspired them or what each of them had loved about him. The ceremony was full and rich with who he was and how he influenced so many lives. Jill and her mother reveled in stories about Jeff's compassionate heart, stories about his sense of humor, stories about how he had enriched so many lives, adding deeper layers to the collage. Everyone laughed and cried as story after story touched on a familiar experience, providing lasting memories for everyone present.

After the service they planned a simple, beautiful burial of Jeff's ashes. Among Jill's many memories were the hours she and Jeff spent as children climbing the neighborhood trees and munching on crisp apples. Jill and her mother found a private park whose owner was willing to receive Jeff's ashes and got permission from the county to bury the ashes under an apple tree they planted themselves. The physical act of shoveling out the heavy soil, feeling the weight of it, and breathing in the rich earthy smell was important. After the hole was dug, they stood in silence for some time, then poured the ashes into the hole. The planting of a living, growing, fruit-giving tree above the ashes was very moving, and the simplicity of it all was appropriate to who Jeff was.

No one need ever be ashamed of parading his or her grief at memorial services or funerals. I believe the growing dissatisfaction with traditional funerals is in part a reaction to maudlin, made-to-order funerary practices. Out of this mold, impersonal services have given rise to the memorial services first championed by the Unitarian Universalists and now generally regarded as appropriate in all but the most orthodox religions.

How does one create a memorial service? It always depends upon the bereaved. The service is for them. It is also for the community. One must not forget them. I always build a service according to the requests of the family. If they are a people of God they get a "Godly service." A humanist, a humanist service. I tailor my service to the needs of the survivors. This involves interviewing family and friends wherever possible and selecting appropriate readings. First I ask to see the whole family or people close to the dead person. This way at the service I do not come as a stranger. I say something like, "Talk to me about Horace. What was he like? What were his interests? How are you feeling? What would you like me to say? Remember this service is for you. Horace is beyond our reach. This is a remembrance, a celebration, a time to think of Horace. Who among you would like to say something at the service? Who outside the family might be asked to have a few words of remembrance? You talk now." I often get notes afterwards saying in effect, " How could you know what I needed to talk about." The answer is: "I know."

–Farley W. Wheelwright, retired Unitarian Universalist clergyperson.

~

BERNICE

When Doug Goslings' mother died, her ceremony was in the Lutheran tradition carefully and thoughtfully tailored to the special person she was. Bernice designed some of her own ritual before she died but left the creation of most of it to her family and her minister.

The minister of their church knew how to help the family choose the right music and the right people to involve in the funeral. Her service included many personal elements that made it meaningful for everyone in attendance. His mother had chosen her own pallbearers. There were six men and two women who actually carried her. She also had honorary pallbearers who were her closest women friends.

Doug has fond memories of his mother's service: "Contrary to a lot of people's experience around funerals, it was not painful. It was actually an amazing experience to be able to get a reflection of who she was by the kinds and numbers of people who came and the kinds of things they said about her. It was a fantastic affirmation of my mother. I didn't find it exhausting. I found it like a high. I felt incredibly energized by it. All of us in the family were really hosts and were actually serving the purpose of returning some of my mother's feelings for them as we met all these people."

Doug's mother was a feminist in the deepest sense, and the minister acknowledged her role in the feminist movement. When he said the

Lord's Prayer he prayed to "our mother who art in heaven." The family also appreciated how he used nongender specific pronouns throughout the ceremony. It brought some of her politics into the ceremony.

By personalizing the traditional ceremony and working with a sensitive minister who knew their mother, the family created an outstanding tribute to their mother.

If the goal of a funeral is to do your best by the person who has died, you might ask yourself how best to accomplish that *before* calling the local mortuary. It's a good idea to have a clear notion of what you do *and* don't want so the funeral industry can't take advantage of indecision. For example, it's easy to be shamed by a mortician into getting a top-end casket even though we know it really has nothing to do with our respect for the dead. It might be much more meaningful to spend the extra money flying in close friends or family rather than on a box that's going to be buried in the ground. And while traditions can bring a certain amount of comfort because they are familiar, don't be afraid to get creative and make some new traditions.

~

JENNY

Catherine McCauley's parents and aunt and uncle were planning their joint fiftieth wedding anniversaries and were going to have a family reunion in Oregon to celebrate. Three weeks before the reunion, Catherine's Aunt Jenny had a stroke and died. The family thought about canceling the reunion but after planning for five years, they decided that rather than abandoning the reunion, they would turn it into a memorial. There were almost fifty family members between the two families and everyone was involved, including several young children. In the end, the memorial service helped provide closure for the whole family.

"My Aunt Jenny was cremated and her ashes put in a ceramic urn," Catherine recalls. "At the memorial service each person was invited to bring something to put in her grave along with her ashes. Since she had been an avid reader, somebody brought the little paperback book she had been reading when she was dying and then talked a little bit about how she enjoyed reading. Jenny was also a gardener, so my cousin brought the mutilated clippers (they had been accidently run over by a truck; she liked to use them anyway), so they went with the ashes into the grave, too. The humor was really a healing addition, providing laughter as well as tears. My aunt made a lot of lists so somebody wrote out a list of things for her to do. Aunt Jenny was buried with all these personal memories from her family surrounding her.

"All the kids gathered around in a circle and in the center there was a purple candle that represented my aunt. Each child had a small white candle they lit from the purple candle. Each one wrote a memory of her on a piece of paper and read it aloud. Then they burned the piece of paper. It was their personal way of saying good-bye. At the end they blew out the candles and my uncle blew out my aunt's candle."

~

PETER

Peter had a long and lingering illness and finally died at his elegant hill-top home overlooking the San Francisco Bay. He was cremated. His children asked Michael, Peter's long-time friend to lead the memorial in their father's home. Michael felt his role was to shape the ceremony and set the tone. Peter had had a wry sense of humor, and Michael tried to keep things light while at the same time allowing people to grieve.

Peter had lived a glamorous and interesting life. He looked and lived like a movie star. He had been a naval academy graduate, a commodore, a professor at Stanford University, a flamenco guitarist, and founder of a successful software company. Michael had arranged ahead of time for people from different periods in Peter's life to say a few words. There were a few stories from his navy days and from his working life, and then his guitar teacher played the lute. There were stories from his days in business, and then a friend from a concert group that Peter helped found played one of Peter's favorite Bach pieces on the piano. A few people spoke spontaneously. One friend recited a special poem Peter had selected a few weeks before his death.

Finally his son read the last passage from his father's personal journal, an insightful self-observation by Peter. The day was warm and clear and more than seventy people came and enjoyed an elegant buffet that was served in the dining room that opened onto the outside deck in the home Peter loved.

~

JAMES

Beth Fox was a very young woman on the day her husband, James, went off to work and never came home. James was only thirty-six when he died without warning, leaving Beth and their two young children, ages three and five. Instead of turning to the death experts, as most people in her circumstance would have done, Beth reached deep into herself and decided to do what she knew was important for her, her children, in-laws, friends, and members of the rural community in which they lived. Beth felt it would be valuable for her children to be part of the creation of a special ritual for their father, and she also respected the concerns and wishes of her in-laws. She had no model to follow but her heart and so she created an especially joyous and caring memorial.

"James was buried in a cemetery near our house. I did it exactly as I wanted to. No one else took over my way to say good-bye to James. I was able to create a place where his friends could say good-bye to him in a respectful, honoring, good way. Not estranged and scary and full of denial. Estrangement is typically what a funeral is like. This was wonderful. Two hundred people gathered under the redwood trees. Cut flowers were everywhere.

"People who knew and loved James got up and spoke. They read poetry. There were people waiting in line to share their thoughts and remembrances about him, what kind of a teacher he was; what kind of a father he was. After that we carried his coffin to the cemetery, which is just down the road here. We all walked behind the coffin. Friends played music. We sang 'Will the Circle Be Unbroken' and some Simon and Garfunkel songs. It had just rained. It was a gorgeous clear sweet morning. The sun was real bright and there were children everywhere. There was something very wholesome about it.

"We had a bowl with floating burning candles and flowers, and we all stood beside the grave and sang more songs as he was being lowered in. We had a group of friends who have incredible voices. It was like angels singing. Everyone buried him. I think we had six or seven shovels. Everyone did some shoveling. The others went back to the house and I stayed there with my son. We continued to bury his father. He was shoveling with his little hands. We stayed there until it was completely finished. Then we came back home."

~

CHRIS

Chris, a high school football hero, died unexpectedly at the age of eighteen. He was so beloved by family and friends, so much a part of his classmates' lives, that his death affected everyone. Students mourned the loss of their friend and in most cases, were confronted for the first time with their own mortality. Twenty-four-hour grief counselors were made available.

Four close friends of Chris' were especially disoriented, sorrowful, and angry. Wally, a Tibetan meditation practitioner, invited the boys to participate in a ceremony at his sanctuary. Wally's wife recalls, "I lit a candle and spoke and then lit my son's candle and he spoke and so on until all of the candles were lit around the circle. We created a healing flame for Chris.

"We brought him into our hearts and minds and felt his presence. We each shared a memory of him, how we felt about him dying. It came from our hearts. Then I had each of the boys choose a tarot card and as a group we spoke about each card and what would help them or block them as they dealt with this loss. We discussed the best thing each could do to foster his own growth and honor Chris's memory. Afterward the boys all looked and felt better, more peaceful. Each boy kept his candle. We all felt we were holding Chris in our hearts for eternity and no longer felt so separate from him. We felt where he was, we all would be going."

There is something about carrying the coffin, composing a poem, singing a special song, even shoveling dirt into a grave that facilitates closure. I can't emphasize enough how playing an active role helps the living. And if organizing or directing aren't your strengths, there are many important activities for you, your friends, and family to participate in. There is decorating the coffin or urn, helping select music or flowers, lighting candles, passing out flowers, sharing stories, or reading poetry. When there is room for everyone to participate actively, the last good-bye takes on a 'high' quality that comes when people get to say their farewells in their own way. There is comfort knowing that the death ceremony was done right, that family and friends truly honored the life of the person who died.

Sometimes this doesn't work out such as when the biological family members are committed to a traditional service and are, for whatever reasons, unwilling to consider any kind of alternative. In that case you might want to improvise or hold a separate ceremony at a future time to meet your needs. All too often the biological family completely ignores the partner and friends of the deceased and whisks the body away to wherever the family came from leaving behind a community of friends with a need to grieve. Holding a separate ceremony makes complete sense in such a case.

When Farley's sister Ruth died, her service was held in the Salvation Army Retirement Hotel where she lived for twenty-five years. The Salvation Army Major insisted upon having their regular service. This may have satisfied the residents in the home, but did nothing for the rest of her friends and immediate family. Farley recalls: "We retired to a near-by apartment and celebrated Ruth's life in our own way: with family remembrances—photos, her silver, stories, and a lovely meal. Our own made-on-the-spot ceremony took away the bad taste of an orthodox service that ground Ruth into the grave instead of exalting her lovely spirit."

P. J. Tyler, an astrologer who deals everyday with people's deepest emotional issues, frequently designs rituals and helps people express their feelings during times of loss. When her father-in-law died, she assumed his service would celebrate and reflect his life, and that her grief could be shared with other friends and relatives. She was very disappointed.

"My father-in-law was really the closest thing to a father I had so I was really anxious to go back to Minnesota and be a part of his memorial service. A singer in the choir and very active in his church, he was given a very traditional Christian ceremony. I couldn't understand it. During the whole service his name was mentioned only a couple of times. He was a larger-than-life, live-out-loud man, who had been important in his community, but the minister never said a word about the man I knew. He was buried in a Veterans' cemetery and when the soldier tried to blow the trumpet it was so cold he couldn't make a peep. The whole thing was all just form. Formula. Completely generic.

"It just wasn't enough. I wanted to talk about Dad and hear stories about his life. I knew I would be catching a plane soon and felt so let down. Fortunately there were others who felt the same way, so after the service we gathered around the Jell-O salads and told stories about the real man we all knew and loved. We glutted ourselves on him."

P. J. did the best she could to have her needs met at the time, but she returned home with a lot of unresolved grief. Because she knew the importance of ritual in healing, she called up a few close friends and

---

~

When Others Are Grieving

To my mind there is only one appropriate action when a person is grieving: weeping along with the person, usually without saying anything. There are times when words seem to belittle intense feelings.

There are many things we ought not to do:

Don't tell a person that grief is inappropriate AND SHOULD NOT be expressed.

Don't tell a person there are still many reasons to rejoice.

Don't speculate about what happens to the deceased. Don't assume that the one grieving shares your conviction about the unknown.

Don't talk about the will of God.

Don't try to comfort with words. Hugs are much better.

---

held a memorial for her father-in-law one evening in her backyard under the stars. She gathered her support group around her, shared stories and photos, sang songs, and lit candles to honor the man who was so influential in her life.

While no one looks forward to the loss of a loved one, grief is not to be avoided but embraced as the route back into life. Nor should other people's grief be squelched or avoided. Because of our own fears of death and loss we tend to try and stifle the pain and grief of others with platitudes like, "Well, his suffering is ended," or, "They are with Grand-

Don't pretend you know the feelings of the person grieving.

Don't suggest that grief is temporary and that time will heal.

Don't suggest that the bereaved one immediately replace the loss.

Don't say, "Let me know if I can do anything." Rather, offer specific suggestions to help.

Don't ask about plans for the future. The present is all the bereaved person can handle.

Don't shun the bereaved person because you don't know what to say. You don't need to say anything. It will be your presence that will comfort.

On the positive side: Be available to the person grieving while sensitive to the need for solitude. Do unto the bereaved what he/she would have you do unto him/her, not what you think is best.

Farley W. Wheelwright

~

mother in heaven now." They may well be in heaven, but you might feel like you're in hell, isolated and alone. Their suffering may indeed be over, but yours is just beginning.

Because each of us is unique, it is not possible to prescribe a single method for dealing with grief. The only general advice I can give is that death is a certainty, and the wise person knows his or her sources of strength before it's time to deal with it. Too often we have not taken the time to acquaint ourselves with our sources of comfort and when the storm strikes we do not know where to turn for refuge.

Special rituals help the living cope with unfinished business or unresolved emotional work in difficult relationships. Instead of merely going through the motions, the following story illustrates how one family pulled together to pay tribute to their mother.

~

BRENDA

Brenda, an English professor, died at the age of fifty-four. She was an alcoholic who smoked two packs of cigarettes a day. She had refused to give up drinking and smoking and finally her body just gave out. She left a lot of unfinished business for her husband, John, and their three children to deal with. Before she died, she told her family she wanted "no funeral and no ceremony, no sloppy sentimental stuff. Just throw my body away."

Her husband was so angry after Brenda died that he was inclined to honor Brenda's wishes and have her cremated without any ceremony. But one of their sons, who had spent a lot of time in Bali and witnessed numerous rituals for the dead, was appalled. He needed a ceremony. He wanted closure and he felt very strongly that tribute be paid to his mother's life. He begged his father to reconsider and his father finally relented.

At first the family had no idea how to go about designing a ceremony, so they got together and started talking about some of the good times Brenda had enjoyed. John remembered a really wonderful trip they had taken to Latin America. He recalled the time they had stopped at a chapel in a small village during a funeral. The chapel had been decorated with hundreds of candles and rose petals and this ritual had touched John and Brenda deeply.

To recreate the feeling of that faraway place, the family rented an old unused church on the outskirts of Boston. The son carved a special doll to put in his mother's coffin and the other family members each brought something personal to place in Brenda's coffin. Because it was winter John had to drive three hours away to a wholesale florist, returning with a carload of roses. The family stripped the petals from the stems and put them into baskets. They bought hundreds of multicolored candles and covered the walls and altars with candles and rose petals. As they worked, they talked about what Brenda had given them that had special meaning in their lives. The process of forgiveness and acceptance had begun. Then they all went together to the crematorium and watched though the viewing window as her body burned.

A few days later they had the memorial service where hundreds of candles were lit and the scent of roses filled the church. Many people who loved Brenda attended the service. No words were planned, people just got up and talked. John, who was usually very shy, got up and spoke with eloquence. Creating something special enabled him to begin to move past his anger at his wife for dying so unnecessarily and to publicly acknowledge his love for her.

A funeral or memorial ritual should be a reflection of the individual. It should express the soul, nature, or essential quality of that person. This can be done in many ways, using media and other creative expressions such as music, song, poetry, storytelling, or mural painting.

Renee Fowler was a warm, vivacious, caring woman who played a central role in her community. Renee loved to dance and sing and she and her husband, Stephen Fowler, were dedicated members of their local choir.

Stephen wrote a poem after Renee's death that was later put to music and performed by the Occidental Community Choir. "Renee had barely been able to walk, much less dance, the last year of her life," Stephen recalls. "For me, the emotional peak of the song is the suggestion that some part of her 'now dances in the breeze.' Even now I cannot write this without tears. Robin Eschner, a choir member, took this phrase, gave it to the altos and sopranos and spun it into a lovely long crescendo. A male chorus sang a drone, and a dulcimer added an antique elegance. The benefit for me in being able to perform this piece with my friends and our daughter, Sarah, was to transcend my grief through its public recognition and the miracle of art, which no amount of weeping in a therapist's office could have given me."

Rituals do not have to be confined only to funeral or memorial services. In many traditions, the dead are honored and remembered yearly. Some of these traditions can be helpful and give you ideas to borrow for your own rituals.

~

My Wife's Trees

Verse 1

We buried the ashes of my wife one day,

Under Madrone and Oak and Bay,

Whose roots reach down to the ashen part

Of the one who taught my ignorant heart to love

Ah, to love!

Verse 2

I softened the soil around the spot

And a daughter planted forget-me-nots,

Whose roots reach down to the ashen part

Of the one who taught my ignorant heart to love

Ah, to love!

Chorus:

Ashes, dust, death, rust,

These are all things that we must trust,

Because fallen leaves make the best nourishment

For new leaves, which now dance in the breeze

High up in the tops of my wife's trees.

—Stephen Fowler

In Mexico two days out of the year are especially devoted to death: November first, known as the Day of All Saints, and November second, dedicated to the Faithful Dead. On these two festival days people celebrate and actually throw parties for the dead. Cemeteries are cleaned up and tombs are painted and decorated with candles and flowers to create an atmosphere of luminescence and celebration. Offerings of favorite dishes, sweets, and local fruits and flowers are placed in the largest room in the house, in hopes that the dead will appreciate the sweet smells and the richness of the gifts. In some places dances are held, fireworks are lit, and local artists create songs, poems, and sculptures as religious offerings for the dead.

Padi Selwyn borrowed a bit of this concept for her grandmother's unveiling. In the Jewish tradition, eleven months after the funeral the family revisits the grave and removes the cloth covering the headstone, which is the unveiling ceremony. Padi's grandmother had loved raspberries, so Padi brought a large bowl of the sweet red fruit to pass among family and friends at the graveside. The berries that weren't eaten were strewn over the grave as part of the service. "This personalized the service and brought my grandmother's memory to us more vividly. Partaking in something that she enjoyed so much brought her closer to us."

Gloria, a Presbyterian woman who lost her four-year-old child in the month of December many years earlier, shared with a rabbi how miserable she always felt around the holiday season. He suggested that one of the Jewish traditions might help. On the anniversary of the death of a loved one, a remembrance candle, known as a Yartzheit candle, is lit and left to burn for twenty-four hours. This time is for remembering the loved one, for sharing stories. Around the New Year, Gloria saw the rabbi again and told him she had taken his suggestion and lit a candle on December 10, the anniversary of her daughter's death. She told him that this was the first year she had actually enjoyed Christmas in fifteen years. Gloria finally had a day when she felt it was appropriate to mourn.

It is my hope that the stories in this chapter may suggest similar rituals to you when faced with the trauma of death. When done with sensitivity and care, a death ritual not only facilitates the healing process, it offers a clear picture of all the person represented. A death ritual done well creates structure and solace. It is life affirming and transformative, providing a rich opportunity to pay tribute to what was unique about the person who died. A well-crafted death ritual is like a well-loved pocket stone, an important memory that we can bring out when we need it.

CHAPTER FIVE

Taking Charge
of Your Own Farewell

There is a quiet transformation in America surrounding our death rituals, as we realize that we have options for our last passage. This is a healthy trend that needs our support, applause, and encouragement. A groundswell of pioneers is creating meaningful alternatives to the traditional rituals accompanying death, ensuring that they have a memorable send-off.

Only 10 percent of the population dies without warning, giving the majority of us plenty of time to plan for the end of life. Most of us choose instead to ignore the subject entirely. In fact, the vast majority of Americans die without a will, let alone instructions for their funeral or memorial service. In addition to tending to the more practical aspects of your life that we discussed in Chapter Two, you might also wish to include guidelines for your memorial service. Planning your own memorial service can be a valuable gift to yourself and to those you love. Thinking about your own farewell—be it flamboyant, reserved, or something in between—is also good practice when it comes time to design ceremonies for others. This is a healthy, liberating exercise not an obsession with death. It is a playful dance with an old enemy. From time to time I contemplate my life in the context of my death ritual by asking myself what matters most to me and what values I want to pass on. I also look at treasures given me by friends, and things I have created or acquired that have special meaning for me. For example, I have lots of art, and I imagine different friends and family members appreciating it after I am gone. I think about what kind of a ceremony might draw my family and friends closer together so they might see how incredible they are. This practice helps keep my life in balance.

Several years ago I began planning my memorial by talking about it with a few close friends. It was strange to talk about at first and, being a bit superstitious, I worried that a lightning bolt would strike me dead then and there. But eventually we all had a good time fantasizing about the details of our rituals. It drew us closer together and gave me support to speak more freely with my family.

The Coffin Garden

As these talks about dying evolved I felt the urge to create a sacred space in my garden. It has become a focal point where it feels natural to hold rituals celebrating both life and death. Everything changes in the garden. Everything is being recycled: The beautiful flowers fade, and the luscious berries are harvested leaving the vines to dry into little sticks that are cut back in the spring to encourage new growth and another crop in the fall.

A lot of the plants end up in the heap with grass clippings, kitchen scraps, and castings from the worm bin, which turns into compost to nourish the next crop of vegetables, berries, fruits, and flowers.

We call this sacred space the coffin garden. There is a gazebo in the middle surrounded by a rock wall filled with flowers. My husband, who is a contractor, made a fiberglass mold from which using a mixture of vermiculite, peat moss, and concrete, we made coffin-shaped planter boxes. Each box overflows with flowers and herbs. Surrounding each coffin box are concrete squares decorated with broken pottery tiles and tiles we have painted ourselves. It was so much fun making the stepping stones that we set up a workspace in the garden and encouraged friends to help us paint a tile or create a stepping stone.

Almost everyone who visits is touched in some way by the garden, so abundant with fruit trees and flowers and surrounded by lavender. Bright gold calendulas, a relative of the marigold family which are the traditional flowers used to adorn Day of the Dead altars, and California poppies and daisies are everywhere. The garden celebrates the life cycle by bringing death nearer to us, continually reminding us that nothing really dies.

Many visitors spontaneously contribute a story, a poem, or a memorable death ceremony. Someone donated a bench in honor of Lou Gottleib, one of the Limeliters and a gifted musician who loved nature. Here visitors can quietly contemplate life and death as they look out over the valley below. An old friend, Donna Freeman, fashioned a sign for the entrance that proclaims *'Bloom Where You're Planted.'* When David, my grandchildren's godfather, died, we planted a bed of flowers in his honor. We made a figure out of wood and painted it in bright colors to represent David and stood it among the flowers. The figure holds a martini in one hand and a pack of cigarettes in the other. When we walk by David's flower bed sometimes we say his name or tell a story. It seems to make the children more relaxed about his death and it keeps his memory alive.

Delia brought over some of her husband's ashes and with her daughter, Amanda, buried the ashes beneath a catalpa tree and planted rosemary for remembrance. I strung some colored beads from the tree branches and painted a wooden star to mark the spot. My friend, Robin, planted some of her mother's ashes beneath a pink pearl apple tree near the asparagus bed, as her mother was quite fond of both. There is an altar in honor of my father, a small pond, prayer flags, a skull covered with small pieces of shiny glass painted in rich hues of blue and orange, and many other artistic contributions.

I am designing a coffin made from willow branches formed in the shape of a swan, as I want to be propped up during my memorial ceremony with those big wings enfolding me. Before my time comes, I hope to use my coffin as a rocking chair in the garden so I am attaching wheels to move it from place to place. I will lie in my swan beneath a lattice-work bower covered with flowers in hues of blues, pinks, and purples gathered that morning from the garden. I will wear a long patchwork gown I am making from old clothes and fabrics that I have been saving for the past ten years (I am a very slow seamstress). After the ceremony I will be wrapped up in a beautiful woven shroud, which we enjoy now as a table covering, and cremated.

I have written in my instructions that I wish my friends and extended family, who are a very talented bunch, to perform little skits, sing songs, tell stories, and play music together. I hope those gathered will sing *'Red River Valley,' 'Eagle When She Flies,'* and *'Will the Circle Be Unbroken'* with gusto.

I won't plan everything in advance, as I enjoy serendipity and wish to encourage my friends to tap into their most creative selves and really appreciate our lives together. Some aspects of the memorial do feel very important to me and I have included them in a letter with my will. I want to give my family and community the opportunity to share in the experience of having an active part in my memorial. As those I love gather to help my spirit pass, I want them to gather strength and joy from this ceremony and to celebrate their own lives.

I used to worry too much about the practical aspects: What if it is the wrong season and the garden isn't in bloom? What if I die in India or some other far away place? What if I am a hundred when I die and my close friends and family have already passed on? I am now learning to let go of the practical details and focus on what I would want if I died right now, knowing it will change as circumstances change. Originally I had rather outlandish fantasies that would in reality be difficult for my family to carry out. As a result of sharing my wishes with my husband and daughter, I have made changes to accommodate their comfort level and I now feel they have a good idea of what matters to me. Basically I hope for an upbeat ceremony with lots of tears and laughter.

From time to time as I stand in my garden, I yell out, "Roll on Death," which I first heard from James Clegg, a marine biologist, who learned it from his dad. His' father and his fellow soldiers would yell "Roll on Death" in the battlefields of World War I to keep up their spirits, and James (and now I) use it to proclaim our aliveness.

Part of the planning and sharing of your send-off is to prepare yourself for death, and part is to inspire your friends and family to make their individual preparations. It's a good way to open up conversations about death so we can start letting go of our fear. Ester B. Fein wrote in *The New York Times*, "Talking in advance about death is clearly no salve for the pain of losing a mother, a child or a friend. But when people avoid the subject, many health care experts say, dying often becomes even more traumatic to patients and those caring for them, compounding the loss that even the most careful planning can never erase."

One of death's greatest gifts is that sometimes when you lose a close friend, his or her exit can cause new relationships to be born or strengthen old ones. Whether we realize it or not, we are the center of a network that needs us emotionally for solace and guidance. When we leave and the circle of friends is missing a member, our friends need to recreate their support system in a new way. A really thoughtful ceremony celebrating your death can function as a way to help heal and to reconfigure your family and friends.

It's easier to face the thought of death when you talk and plan with others. I have found that most people are relieved to talk about death with someone other than their lawyer or accountant. Psychologist and author Kathleen Dowling Singh notes in her book *The Grace in Dying*, "The imagery in which we as a culture conceive of death and dying has shifted subtly in the last few decades. It is moving from images on enclosing darkness to images of expansive radiance. Our images of death are, increasingly, filled with light. Dying is moving out of whispered shadows and into open-eyed sharing."

In this chapter, I ask you to consider the creation of your final ritual as a parting gift to yourself and your loved ones. I realize that planning your own service may not be for everyone. Some of you may be perfectly content and relieved to let someone else take control of your final exit. You may want to leave a simple note with your will that states that funeral arrangements are not important to you.

Perhaps you feel a traditional service will suit you just fine. You might feel you're not adventurous enough or bold enough to design your own good-bye at this time. Perhaps you worry that some of your friends or relatives may be put off or that it will embarrass your children. If you have any of these feelings, I encourage you to read this chapter anyway, to learn why others have chosen to take charge of their final ceremony.

It's not easy to pioneer in an area so seldom dealt with in an open and direct way. In this case the rewards are well worth any risk.

Increasingly, people are leaving instructions for their service along with their will and other important papers to make sure their wishes are clear to their survivors. This reminder of your wishes can be especially helpful at a time when people are in pain and overwhelmed. We have all heard horror stories or been involved in our own nightmares as people hassle and bicker over their interpretation of the wishes of those who can no longer speak for themselves. If it's all written down, then there is no confusion about whether to bury or cremate, invite the world in or have a private ceremony. The people left behind will be assured they are honoring your wishes.

When you have it spelled out there is more time for coping and comforting each other and less time trying to figure out "what he or she would have wanted." This can only enhance their peace of mind and help alleviate stress and confusion during a difficult time.

Bay Area artist Madeleine Fitzpatrick tells us why creating a hand-crafted ritual can be so special: "I've gone to gatherings where you leave as though you had been to a wedding. You leave high, over-whelmed with joy that you knew this person. And you tell everybody 'I was just at the most inspiring funeral in the world—and I am just high for life!" That's the way powerful death rituals can affect people. The ceremony can uplift your spirits and give you a far greater appre-ciation for the incredible gifts you have in your life. It can also serve as a wake-up call to enrich your own life, motivating you to make your dreams real *now*.

Ideally, part of putting your life in order will include designing some, if not all, of your own memorial service—it ends all ambiguity about what, where, and when. Many people feel that planning their own memorial has enriched their lives. It is a valuable gift they are giving to themselves as well as to those they love. They feel it's important to take charge of the sacred events that define their life.

Here are a few ideas to help you start thinking about the kind of ritual that feels appropriate to you.

Epitaph

Write your epitaph. This is a challenging exercise, as you only get a few words to sum up your entire life. If your life seems too beige, you still have time to fill it up with rainbows. Every year, perhaps on your birthday, review your epitaph and see how it's changed. Refine what you've written.

Jude Winerip Mariah did a paper on gravestones for a class on death at her local junior college and decided to design her own. Her lover carved it for her. Jude wrote her epitaph and thought about who she wanted to come to her funeral and what she wanted said. Jude laughs as she remembers, "I teased my friends and told them I wanted to be the disc jockey at my own funeral, so I have all the music picked out—you will be hearing everything from Bette Midler to Louis Armstrong. I realized that the most important part for me is I want people to leave me and me to leave them with a sense of knowing who I am and being able to thank them for being in my life."

Coffin

You might want to make your own coffin or order one from one of the suppliers listed in the Resource section. One of my friends uses her coffin as a coffee table and from time to time lies inside as she feels this helps her overcome her fear of dying. She also finds talking about death helps her face the inevitable and having a coffin coffee table is certainly a conversation starter!

There are very inexpensive cardboard coffins available from one of the many vendors listed in the Resource section. These come folded for easy storage, and some people like the idea of having one on hand for the convenience of their survivors.

Funerary Urn

I have invited people to contribute love tokens in the form of a jewel, poem, rock, button, or piece of ceramic to put in my funerary urn. I love the idea of my ashes residing in this special spirit vessel surrounded by these small gifts from my friends and family. The urn itself was made in Indonesia and sits at the end of our dining room table.

You might want to make an urn for your ashes out of modeling clay, play dough, or Sculpie, or to get ambitious and sculpt one yourself. Or ask your friends to help you embellish a ready-made spirit vessel that can be used as a vase now and, later, to hold your ashes.

Ashes to Ashes

There are many poignant and even humorous stories about people's requests for disposing of their ashes. Ashes have been put into bullets and shot into favorite hunting spots. They have been put into tobacco humidors, cameras, cookie jars, bowling pins, and duck hunting decoys. They have been scattered from airplanes and hot air balloons and over the grave of a favorite pet. Handcrafted hollow pendants have been filled with cremated remains. Ashes have been mixed with a ceramic glaze and fired onto the surface of a treasured pot.

John, a neighbor of mine, loved antique cars. When John died, his family put his ashes into a prized racing cup that they keep in the back seat of his lovingly restored 1939 Ford Roadster. At least twice a year the family drives the Ford to John's favorite antique car gathering and invites his friends to sit in the back seat with the urn.

A pyrotechnician who wanted to go out as a giant firecracker requested that his ashes be rolled up into a big round shell that exploded into brightly colored stars at a fireworks convention. Gene Roddenberry and Timothy Leary enjoyed a space funeral, complete with a Pegasus rocket that carried some of their ashes in a small aluminum capsule that was blasted into orbit.

Some people leave minimal instructions, such as "scatter my ashes at sea," or "bury me under a rose bush." Others leave very detailed instructions about what they want: whom to ask, favorite music to be played, the kind of flowers, the clothes they want to be buried in, who the pall-bearers should be, etc.

Still others have fantasies that they hope can be carried out when they die that are not at present possible because of current legal considerations. The reforms occurring within the funeral industry and the rise in alternative memorials and funerals ensure that our choices will expand considerably in the next decade.

Bronwyn has her fantasy death in mind: "My wish would be to have my husband and daughter floating me in the pool at Harbin Hot Springs in Northern California. They would hold me and I would be floating in warm water looking up at a wonderful overarching fig tree with the light coming through the leaves. That would be the most beautiful passage. We do that with babies . . . we water birth babies . . . we can water death people." Maybe someday, Bronwyn.

Hanya Parker grew up in the United States but was raised by grandparents from Russia on a farming commune in Arizona centered around their church. "I remember some of the old rituals but my memory is from when I was a young person, as I left the church in my early twenties. When a person died, I know they held a vigil so there would always be someone there with the deceased. The house would be open all the time for people to come and visit. I would like to have that incorporated into my ritual. On the third day, they made a procession with singing and prayers as they carried the coffin to the cemetery. Everyone at the funeral was dressed in white, which I think is another lovely idea.

"I can go there now and see where my mother and grandparents and aunts and uncles are buried—everybody is in one place and that's really nice. Some part of me would like to be buried with them, but right now I feel I would like to be buried at home. I want to wear a simple white dress and I don't want shoes. One of the rituals that I would like to carry over from my heritage is the love feast—the breaking of bread together. I want a long table with a white tablecloth on it and I want this all outside. I want my friends and family to sing some sad songs and then lots of happy ones.

"I hope by the time I die that I can be planted near my beloved fruit trees, vegetables, and flowers. I would like to be covered in flower blossoms all over my dress and in my hair. I hate when you go to cemeteries, the casket is there, you say some prayers and hug and kiss everybody and then you walk away. I want to be lowered into the ground. I want to be actually physically planted. And I want my friends to do it."

Hanya's life is about sharing the beauty of the environment through her landscape paintings and creating a spectacular garden. Her ritual is a natural extension of what's important to her. Even if she can't be buried in her own garden because of legal issues, it is clear to her family and friends about the type of ceremony she wants.

Hanya was inspired to create her own ritual by her art professor, Bill Morehouse, whose knowledge of his impending death gave him the impetus and opportunity to create his own good-bye. With the help of his wife, friends, colleagues (including many well known artists), and caregivers, Bill had invitations sent out inviting people to come to his studio to paint a magic square on his handmade coffin or to send something to be included with him in cremation. Mail came from all over the world and included everything from a scrimshaw peace pipe to a detailed ceramic replica of the ace of hearts. Over a period of a few months this simple wooden box was transformed into an incredibly beautiful and complex work of art. Somebody painted a boat to help Bill on his voyage. Another artist painted a very abstract celestial map with dancing figures around the top. His wife, Michele, painted a house of clouds where he could live and dream. His best friend painted the entire music and words to the "Streets of Laredo" (Bill loved to sing that song!). Tools were painted to help him build life in the next realm. There were windows painted for him to look through and manuscripts to read. His son, Mark, simply wrote "I love you, Bill," on the bottom of the coffin; words that had been so hard to say out loud were one of the most joyous and lovingly uncomplicated statements. Before Bill's cremation, the coffin was documented, photographed, and displayed for an evening celebration at Sonoma

State University in Northern California where Bill had taught for so many years.

Beside Bill's bed were all the little gifts of poetry, tapes, shells, and photos that friends brought to him in his last months. He asked that they all be placed in his coffin with him so that they would become part of his ashes. Bill learned that with the proper county-issued license anyone could drive a loved one to be buried or cremated, so he asked his friend Joy to "accompany" him to the crematorium and to stay with him while he was cremated. He didn't especially like the idea of being "carted off," so Joy drove him to the Neptune Society and lovingly guarded him. Being a Scotsman, Bill just loved that this way it only cost $160!

I had loved and admired Bill for years and attended the memorial service held on a wind-swept California coast. We sang *Amazing Grace* and then off in the distance we heard the haunting sounds of the bagpipe Bill had arranged the month before he died. The musician had even rehearsed the special selections while visiting Bill on his deathbed.

People who wanted to speak did, and then Michele invited everyone to help with scattering his ashes. Hanya recalls: "The wind wasn't really blowing until we were ready to toss the ashes out and all of a sudden the wind blew the ashes right back at us. It was great! At the end, we were hugging each other and the next thing we knew we had palm prints of ashes on our clothes and people were saying 'I'll never take this to the cleaners now.'"

Bill was an inspiration to so many people who continue to talk of his death ritual years later. We had the good fortune of helping to create the good-bye Bill wanted. For Bill, the process of living with his coffin helped him come to terms with his death and tempered some of his fear. He was a teacher to many of us in his life, and in his dying he demonstrated just how precious life is.

A fine printmaker, watercolorist, and beloved teacher, Elizabeth Quandt, planned a very elaborate and formal memorial service in an auditorium at a local junior college. The ceremony included a tea party in a nearby art gallery where exquisite books which she had hand-crafted during her career as an artist were displayed. In addition to a small ensemble of singers who sang some wonderful classical pieces, Elizabeth asked a dear friend to play selected piano pieces. Other friends and family read carefully chosen poems that held deep meaning for Elizabeth and had served as inspiration for much of her artistic creation.

Elizabeth's daughter, Kristina, said that her mother had lived a "complicated life and had played strong and very different roles in people's lives. It felt important to honor her passing and not rob people of their individual experience, to have each person there walk away feeling the story was told that everyone needed to hear."

But of all the performances, the most powerful was at the end of the service when her son, Ward, played a recording she had made from her deathbed. It was Elizabeth in her own soulful voice reciting the William Butler Yeats poem, *The Wild Swans it Coole*.

You don't have to be an artist to create your own ritual. In this era of great change I predict that as with other sacred passages, our death consciousness will rapidly unfold. As more people begin to create their own send-off, others will follow and we will all become more comfortable with death.

Rituals don't have to be elaborate nor do they have to be part of the dying process itself as Bill and Elizabeth's were. If you are not dealing with a terminal illness, your thoughts and desires about your final send-off will probably go through many transformations. I encourage you to write down your thoughts and talk about your wishes with your loved ones as they change.

Richard didn't want a ceremony of any kind but he still wanted to take charge of his own send-off, so he left very detailed instructions to be carried out upon his death. At the reading of his will select friends were called together, most of whom had never met before. They represented various careers and places he had lived and different time periods in his life. Having no close relatives or children, Richard explained in his will that he wanted his six figure estate spent on sending his group of friends on an all expenses paid trip on the Orient Express!

Because he loved to travel first class and took such delight in the friends who had enriched his life, Richard had the joy of envisioning their trip and imagined friendships blossoming. Nearly a year after his death, his friends made the journey together. It was a great tribute to their friend, and following his generous wish was their way of honoring the life of a man who loved to travel and create special gatherings for the people he cared about.

For Madeleine Fitzpatrick, directing her own funeral is very important. Madeleine lives her life fully and enthusiastically and brings this same joyful attitude to planning her own memorial. "At my funeral I'm going to have the most fantastic belly dancer. And great food. I just want everyone to have a wonderful time. I would like a hearse made into an angel and painted with wings coming out of it. I have chosen incredible music. Circle energy is nice. I like the idea of a talking stick. But instead of a stick it would be something personal to me. It would have my energy. Something that would be close and very dear to me. And it would be handed around to everybody who wants to say something. I also have all my clothes that I want to wear picked out if I should die immediately."

Carole wants to be laid out on rose petals and lavender blossoms, with a blue silk pillow filled with moss under her head in the flying turtle boat she had made for her coffin. Her boat will be set in front of her blazing fireplace with candles everywhere for light. At the wake, her friends will have a chance to write or paint on postcards, and (if they are comfortable with doing so) touch her and offer their card to go with her on her journey. Carole keeps an updated copy of her wishes in her boat, along with how she wants her ashes to be distributed so her friends and family don't have to fret over finding her instructions.

Carole, whose business card reads 'Live Art' states: "The main reason for making my wishes clear is to help dispel the taboo our culture has about death and our dark sides. I expect our lack of comfort around death contributes as well to our lack of value for living timely, honest, meaningful lives."

What's important about creating your personal ritual is that it is a reflection of you and your life, and that it helps the mourners celebrate what made you unique. Be as wild or as tame as you want in your imaginings, and then discuss your ideas with those you hold dear. You may want to send out an information packet about death copied from this book and invite your friends to help you talk about what's meaningful by participating in the creation of personal rituals for all of you. Just discussing your ideas can be liberating, and the process will draw those you love closer to you. They might very well help you embellish your ideas, or you might inspire them to design their own send-off. To make sure your fantasy can become reality you can check out the legal requirements in your area by calling your closest Funeral Consumers Alliance. See the Resource section for more information.

When Rabbi Robinson's teenage son, Joel, died in an accident, he asked friends and family for two things at the funeral: "Hug me and tell Joel stories." He explains, "As close as you are with your spouse, child, or dear friend, they spend hours away from you. When someone tells a story they bring you a piece of them that you never had before. Everybody sees your loved one in different situations. Everyone can bring you a piece from that person's life. It is an incredible gift."

You can create a ritual that will knit together the multiple facets of your life and provide closure for those left behind. As family and friends from various parts of your life gather to remember you, this may be the only time they will hear about all of the aspects of your life. For the first time there can be a complete picture of you, and you will have helped to orchestrate it.

Here are some questions to ask yourself when planning your own send-off:

1. Do you want to be buried or cremated? Open or closed casket? Do you plan to be an organ donor and/or donate your body for scientific research? Would you like a handmade or decorated coffin? What about your ashes? Do you want them scattered from a mountaintop or in a 'scatter garden'? Or do you want your ashes divided and given to many friends to scatter or plant in their own memorial gardens? Do you wish to have the memorial service or funeral graveside, at a funeral parlor, or elsewhere? Is there a special place that is meaningful to you? A garden, or a grove of trees, the beach, your home?

2. Are there any clothes that you especially want to wear? Do you want to write your obituary or have someone prepare one in advance? Do you want some special words to mark your grave? Do you want a sculptor to create your own personal marker?

3. Are there favorite works of literature, stories you want told, pieces of music or art you would like included in the service? Do you want to include any or all of the following in your service:

∽ A tape-recorded or video message from you to loved ones.

∽ Photo albums or special photos.

∽ Personal treasures that are symbols of your life, e.g., a collection of bells or beads, shrines, a favorite piece of clothing or hat you are known for, bowls of favorite candy, flowers, etc.

∽ Are there special rituals you would like included, e.g., lighting candles or incense, shoveling dirt, washing of hands, being in a circle, dancing, singing selected songs, planting trees or flowers, painting a group mural?

4. Are there special roles you would like friends or family members to play? Do you want your loved ones to prepare your body, and if so, who? Do you want pallbearers? Whom do you want involved in coordinating the service and participating in it? Do you want a notice in the paper? Do you want your service open to the public?

5. What is the feeling you want to create: A joyous outside event with a jazz band or chamber music indoors; potluck at home with your family and a few close friends looking over photo albums together? What time of day do you want the service? Should it be a nighttime

event with a string quartet or a morning sunrise, or maybe a canoe trip up your favorite river with friends singing in the fading afternoon light?

Sharing the why of your choices can be helpful for your family members. It makes them an active part of the ritual and gives guidance, connection, and comfort while clarifying your wishes.

When you invite the participation of those you love, it facilitates closure by giving them something positive to do for you. It can be something as simple as shoveling dirt into the grave, playing music, picking flowers, lighting candles, sharing stories, or reading poetry. By making room for everyone who wants to actively participate, the last ritual takes on a celebrational quality and the survivors feel satisfied that everything possible was done to honor the passing of a life. Active participation also helps diminish fear. The more open we are about all aspects of dying, the more we can accept death as a natural part of life.

In the spirit of living life to its fullest, planning a memorial for yourself is a marvelous opportunity to make a statement about life—your life. It's your chance to put your essence out there for all to appreciate, understand, remember, and even applaud! After all, to design a send-off that closely mirrors your contributions and beliefs is to leave your message in a concise form that can be enjoyed by the living. Since you have the choice, wouldn't you prefer to be eulogized and memorialized in a creative and meaningful way?

It is empowering to take charge of the sacred events that define your life. Ritual is validating and reassuring. Let your good-bye be a special gift that reassures your loved ones that you had a good life and that provides them with a sense of well-being and closure. I encourage you to discuss your choices with those you love, both to solicit their ideas and feedback and to promote more communication about death itself. The benefits extend far beyond you and your intimate circle. By having the courage to plan your own send-off, you are helping to shape the way our culture honors the dead.

Caring for Your Own

Michele was in the last stages of pancreatic cancer, and I entered her cabin with much trepidation. I practically tiptoed into her room. We had never met and she was in the last precious weeks of her life. Michele was dying and I went to interview her for this book. There was an electric and immediate connection—we became instant friends. We could easily have been sisters and it made us both sad because there was so little time for our friendship to grow. Michele lived straight from her heart.

Several weeks earlier I had seen photos of Michele in the newspaper in a moving article written by Susan Swartz. The headline read: "Orchestrating Her Final Days, on Own Terms" and in smaller type, "Guerneville cancer patient directs final plans including at-home rites." And above that a quote that I find particularly compelling, "I was in control of my life, and I want to be in control of my death."

Both her pain and strength leapt at me from the page. I couldn't stop looking at her. You could see that she was very thin and physically weak. Yet there she was arranging her ceremony and all of the practical aspects of her death. Jerri Lyons and Janelle VaMelvin of the Natural

Death Care Project were shown in the article as they guided Michele through the practical and spiritual maze of her final arrangements. The newspaper was charting unusual territory here. Her dying became an important community event as she had her last days documented in such a public manner. Michele lived her totally honest and open death for us all to witness and be part of. She held court every day from her bed, morphine dripping into her arm, the phone at her elbow, friends coming and going, the beautifully decorated cardboard coffin waiting for her. She was determined to remain in charge until the end. There was no nonsense, no small talk as Michele planned every detail of her death ceremony. The black velvet dress she decided to wear was hanging on the door so she could see it without turning her head. The incredible necklace of blue, red, and gold Egyptian beads was in the sarcophagus coffin in the living room along with her rings and bracelets and a pair of earrings.

I came to be with Michele the day of her funeral. I held her cool, slender feet in my warm hands. Her toenails were painted purple to match the satin lining of her coffin. A gold chain encircled her right toe. On her left ankle was painted a boat to ferry her on her journey. She followed an ancient Egyptian religion, and there were religious artifacts everywhere. Michele was covered in rose petals, her skin pearly and translucent. I took photos so I will never forget. I put glitter on her feet. She was radiant in death and I saw the woman she was before all the pain of disease invaded her body. As the day went on and family and friends came and went, her face relaxed more and more. She was grace. She was a blessing. She was our Egyptian princess.

The front door of her cabin was painted red and hung with a wreath of bay leaves intertwined with purple statice shaped like a heart. In the middle was a doorknocker of a man and woman kissing, reminding me of the love and support Michele's husband Brad had given to help her create her ceremony.

It was a very hot July day, but Michele was cool and at rest in her coffin. Purple cornflowers were draped around her head and gold stars were scattered in her hair. Her necklace was around her neck just as she had envisioned. She was wearing her black dress and surrounded by tarot cards and favorite objects to take with her to her next life. All the tension and pain and worry were gone. Michele was truly at peace.

I saw Susan Swartz, the innovative and talented syndicated columnist from the *Press Democrat* who first introduced me to Michele. She was interviewing people, taking notes for her article about this incredible day. She was working, yet she was fully there for Michele as well. Annie Wells, the Pulitzer Prize-winning photographer, was also there recording the ceremony just as Michele wanted.

We all took turns being with Michele in her room. We touched her, talked with her, and spoke quietly with one other. We rejoice that she is free of pain now and appreciate the gift she has given us—the ultimate gift of herself.

It is only in the last hundred years that we have hired professionals to deal with our dead. For American settlers, death was a constant companion and a part of daily life. People usually died at home, their bodies washed and dressed by the family. The body was laid out in the parlor for a few days, and the children experienced the intimacy of death.

When a child was born, many families stored away a bottle of wine to be opened for the child's wedding toast or funeral eulogy, whichever came first. Families kept a set of burial clothes at the ready and prepared the body at home, watching over it from death to burial. Death was a natural part of life.

Around the turn of the century professionals began to take over the function of the family, creating an entire industry to arrange funerals and care for the dead. Rules and regulations began to dictate every aspect of the dying process. Procedures replaced natural impulses. Bathing and dressing the body, once considered a normal family responsibility, evolved into something foreign, even frightening. According to a 1998 Gallup Poll on death and dying, 87 percent of Americans hope to die at home, yet 80 percent of the population actually die in hospitals or nursing homes, often alone.

Elisabeth Kübler-Ross paved the way for the current end of life and after death renaissance. When I re-read her books I am always impressed with her wisdom. I no longer recall which of her many books the following quote came from, but her message is vitally important. "We routinely shelter children from death and dying, thinking we are protecting them from harm. But it is clear that we do them a disservice by depriving them of the experience. By making death and dying a taboo subject and keeping children away from people who are dying or who have died, we create fear that need not be there. When a person dies, we 'help' their loved ones by doing things for them, being cheerful, and fixing up the body so it looks 'natural.' Again, our 'help' is not helpful; it is destructive. When someone dies, it is important that those close to him participate in the process; it will help them in their grief, and it will help them face their own death more easily."

Many adults in our culture have never seen a dead body. Children are usually isolated and "shielded" from the death of a family member or close friend of the family. The body once cared for and laid out for neighbors and friends to say their good-byes bears no resemblance to the dead bodies our children have grown up seeing on TV and in the movies. It's not surprising then that when someone dies we don't know what to do because we never learned how. Death is no longer a natural part of our lives.

Most of us think of death as violent and removed from our daily lives, something that occurs on the evening news and in the movies and, hopefully, less often in our schools, workplaces, and on our neighborhood streets. No wonder we feel helpless and frightened when confronted with a dead body or when we contemplate our own death.

The corpse is the ultimate symbol of death. There is, of course, no alternative to death but there are alternatives to the way we care for our dead. Being able to touch and personally care for the dead body of someone you love can be a natural extension of the regard you held for them while they were alive. If you are concerned about having a body in your home, remember, it's the same body as it was when alive, the spirit has just moved on. Care for the dead body with the respect and care you gave to the alive body.

When someone close to you dies, your inclination may be to stay with them as their spirit leaves. You may intuitively feel this personal connection is the right thing for you to do, but other powerful messages intrude. Many of us think of death as an emergency. We have been conditioned to be dependent on professionals and feel that caring for a dead body is beyond our ability. We may feel panicky and anxious when someone is dying, and think it's a rule or even a law to immediately call for help. An expected death at home is *not* an emergency and you *don't* have to immediately call the fire department, sheriff, coroner, undertaker, mortician, police, or funeral home. You can take your time. The body won't start to decompose for at least twenty-four hours even if it's summer. There is always plenty of help from all sorts of experts just a phone call away if you feel that you need it.

Remember, once you call a funeral director they will spring into action and whisk the body away. The same is true with the paramedics if you call 911. They have their own rules and you will now be part of their system. If the person dies at home after an illness, his or her physician will at some point have to pronounce them dead and sign a death certificate for legal reasons. But that doesn't have to happen immediately. You can take your time. Contrary to what we see on TV and in the movies, an expected, at home death, *there is no rush.*

If you loved the person and were with them when they died, then *you are the expert about what is right for this person at this time.* You have choices. You can call in all of the intimate loving support you want. Friends and family will be there to help you. If you feel comfortable calling a funeral home and putting everything into their hands, that's fine. If you feel it's right for you to take charge of all funeral arrangements including anointing and preparing the body, that's fine, too. Usually when people recognize they have options they decide on something in between. This chapter is about making the right choice for you and your family.

In my community, after the articles about Michele appeared in the newspaper, people began to investigate the range of options available to them. In the state of California where I live, as in most states, you can create a home funeral and care for your own dead. (Check the Resource section for contact information for Funeral Consumers Alliance, for rules and regulations for your state.) Other options include purchasing or building an economical wood coffin or even one of cardboard and decorating it yourself. The body can lie in honor at home so people can say good-bye in a leisurely manner. You can design your own funeral service or memorial ritual, and in most places you can transport the body to the crematorium.

Caring for the body, while not for everyone, is an option to consider and one that more people are choosing instead of giving that privilege over to a stranger. Preparing the body can help create bonds between the survivors. Some of you might already have had the opportunity of helping to lay out the body of a relative or close friend. Perhaps this is something you wished you could have done for a loved one and now hope will be done for you. I would consider it a sacred honor to be included in the preparation of the body of someone close to me and hope when I die I will be lovingly prepared by those who love me rather than a stranger. I personally believe that the spirit is nurtured by the care and tending of the body during the three days immediately after death and helps to create an easier transition. It gives the living time to continue to care and tend to those they love and to experience the finality of their existence.

In *Alison's Gift*, author Pat Hogan tells the story of a little girl's tragic death and the impact her death had on her community. Hogan recounts how Alison's mother responded to the loss of her child. "From the deepest level of her soul, Beth brought an awareness and beauty to Alison's passing. Beth was blessed with choice and there was a certain magic in that choice. There was magic in a community gathering at a home in support and love, and beauty in rituals such as the funeral service and the around-the-clock vigil. There was magic in what is nearly taboo in our culture, handling death, both physically and emotionally, in a direct and loving manner. There was magic and beauty in creating an environment for comprehending and experiencing the mysteries of life.

"Beth was aware of what she wanted and created an experience that truly honored Alison. In Alison's death, wake, funeral, and cremation, there was grief and joy, loss and growth, silence and singing, and reflection and sharing. Living and dying stood side by side. At heart, Alison's journey is one of transformation, which has touched the lives of many.

"At the time of the accident, Beth's relationship to Alison was foremost in her heart and mind. Beth had an inner clarity and outer resolve. She fulfilled this relationship both spiritually and physically by her care of Alison. Beth saw to Alison's every need right up until the end when she had to surrender her to the fire. She felt a responsibility for Alison's well-being that included body, mind, and soul, and was there as long as Alison needed care in any way. Beth did not want to delegate any of this care to strangers: she brought Alison into this world and she would escort her out as well. This experience has brought Beth peace and consolation. Also, by opening her home and her life to others, Beth allowed hundreds of people a similar participatory experience."

Beth Sanders established Crossings: Caring for Our Own at Death, a nonprofit charitable corporation that provides educational and inspirational materials and services for those who need spiritual, emotional, physical, and practical guidance at the time of death. See the Resource section in the back of the book for more information.

Death rituals are meant to draw people together, to help them grieve. People want to honor your wishes, but preparing your body might be an honor for one and too uncomfortable for another. It's important that you talk through why you want those you love to take care of your body and to put it in writing so there can be no question about your wishes. It's also a good idea to let other family members and intimate friends know now that this is part of your plan and to encourage discussion. Even though "laying out the body" is a nearly forgotten custom, resistance usually gives way to acceptance once it is made clear that this is important to you.

Amy Hill was part of a community support group for her friend and employer, Nancy, who was dying of cancer. Amy had never before worked with a dying person, yet when Nancy died, participated in the process of laying out her friend, since this was what Nancy requested. Amy remembers the experience: "She died at home. I'd been to funerals where I saw people lying in a casket but I never had the chance to hold the hand of someone who had died. For me it was a great demystifying process. It was very liberating without the funeral home, without the casket, without everything all laid out and formal. It was so nice to be able to just give her a kiss and say good-bye. It was very important to me. Her parents allowed her friends to have their private ritual and then they held a traditional Jewish ceremony in a nearby cemetery. Afterwards we all gathered at a friend's home to tell Nancy stories and to share food together."

Karen Leonard is the executive director of the Redwood Funeral Society, one of more than 140 nonprofit consumer groups located throughout the United States and affiliated with the national organization, the Funeral Consumers Alliance. A feisty and brilliant woman, Karen has been a constant source of information and inspiration as well as an effective advocate and erudite spokesperson for the right of people to take charge of their own after death arrangements and for consumer protection. Research assistant for the late Jessica Mitford, she is as spunky and outspoken as her mentor.

Karen notes, "We worship professionalism. We worship technology. We are the only society that takes something that would be a natural process like grief and markets it. When you die, a funeral director purchases a grief packet from a marketing corporation called the Afterloss Program. The program provides pamphlets and newsletters that the funeral director uses to advertise his funeral home. Today bereavement and grief counseling are the job of the funeral director.

"Most people have never actually seen a dead body. We are afraid of dead bodies as though they are contaminated and dirty and we might catch death from them. When I've suggested to people to wait until morning to call the funeral director to save the $100 they have to charge to come out at night, the response is usually, "Oh no, I wouldn't want Mother in the house overnight—dead!" These are people who have taken care of Mother as she was dying and yet they feel a threat from her dead body.

"The only time most of us see bodies is at a funeral where the body has been completely drained and replaced with embalming fluid and wax and made up to look like a life-like dummy. There is no more than about 50 percent of the real body left.

"In other cultures people are actively engaged in preparing for the funeral. Here we call our local funeral director and write out a check and that's about it. The only participation we have is 'Do you want the blue casket or do you want the gold?'"

The following stories are about home funerals to inspire you should you consider this as an option.

~

MARI

Mari was forty-three and had breast cancer. Ellen Galford, her spiritual advisor and death midwife, spent months helping her die. During the process she grew extremely close to both Mari and her husband Tom.

"Mari's husband and I spent three and a half hours preparing her body," Ellen Galford recalls, "And in the process he shared very precious memories about their very intense, loving relationship. Tom told me when she became too weak to accompany him outside he would sit with her, they would look into each other's eyes, and he would say, 'Okay, I'm going to take you outside with me now for a walk with the dog. You can see the fields through my eyes.' He would walk in the field with the dog talking to her from his mind, and then he'd come back and they would talk about the walk in the field.

"When Mari died Tom knew she really wasn't there anymore yet he was so gentle and loving and sweet and compassionate, and so open and so beautiful with her. When it was time to choose her dress Tom said, 'Well, she's going to heaven . . . what's the most heavenly thing? When we were first courting I bought her this silk dress and she loved it and she wore it a lot. I think she should wear that.' He held her feet and said, 'Oh sweetie, I've always loved your feet.'

"It was a really good process for both of us to be with her and to talk to her. Feeling as if she were still there. That she could still hear, yet knowing that she was really gone. People say that the hearing is what leaves last so if you want to talk to somebody you can still speak to them from your heart.

"It was such a process to be with Mari's body and to feel the energy in the room. The rest of the family and friends came up and sat with Mari and immediately felt better. Her radiance filled the room. It was definitely a sacred place. It became a celebration of the joys of her life. People were beautifully affected. They could sit on the bed next to her. They could lay down and put their head on her shoulder if they wanted to. They could touch her. They could put a flower in her hand. They could cry if they wanted. They could do whatever they wanted to do. It was as if they were being spiritually fed when they were with her.

"The women decorated her dresser and put flowers and candles around. Mari loved flowers and probably a hundred thousand rose petals showed up, so we made a bed of rose petals. This was a two-day process.

"You have to, at a certain point, put the top on the box. We were definitely in process about this. Everybody participated. Mari had things the way she wanted them at her final good-bye."

Imagine

You have created instructions for how your death care is to be handled.

There is no panic about what to do or who to call.

Your body being touched with respect and caring.

Imagine your loved ones saying Good-bye to you in a way that would ease their fear about dying.

Your death could be painful yet inspire a celebration of life.

Family and friends being transformed in life through caring for you in death.

People who hold sacred the time of death.

Imagine your death as a heart felt story shared and retold for future generations.

From the brochure of The Natural Death Care Project, Sebastopol, CA.

~

MELISSA AND ROB

Sue Brown was trained at Home Hospice and had been a bereavement volunteer, caregiver, social worker, trainer, and speaker about death. When her daughter, Melissa and her husband Rob were killed by a drunk driver, she knew right away the things that she needed and wanted to do.

"Melissa wasn't yet twenty-nine. She and her husband were both killed instantly. They had been married just three years.

"I needed to see her body and I wanted to dress her myself. I knew from experience that I was entitled to do that and I felt ferocious about it, yet was hesitant about telling even my closest family that I wanted to dress Melissa because I didn't know how they would react. I felt so raw and so vulnerable. As it turned out, everyone was supportive, wonderful.

"When we went to the mortuary, Chester, the funeral director, who is a dear man, was worried. "They don't look so good ... you just need to know," he told me. I didn't care. I wanted to see Melissa.

"My sister-in-law Robin, my daughter Jessica, my step-daughters and Robin's daughter Rebecca, all gathered in the mortuary room. I had brought a dress from Melissa's closet, along with stockings, shoes, and earrings. All of the accoutrements. I had brought a paper bag; I thought that I might be sick.

"When they brought Melissa in on the gurney, she was in a hospital gown. She did not look very bruised and her body was deceptively

~

For This Journey

We are not supposed to be here

where they speak only euphemese,

here in this room of stainless sinks,

strange instruments and acrid chemicals

for preservation, but have persuaded them

to let this husband, father, lover,

dear companion, be bathed and dressed

by known, loved hands.

We are not prepared, who could be,

for this, this silent stranger, sheet draped,

refrigerator cold, skin mottled bluish gray.

I warm your face between my hands,

your lips with mine.

Folds of your neck are pink, soft, partly thawed.

Their living texture shocks.

I know this skin, these folds, stroke them,

shut out the room, pretend.

You are made ready as you would have wished.

A favorite sweatshirt, worn khakis, two-for-

one-price sneaks (you called them "spiffy")

and in your hands the battered, stained safari hat

that traveled with you on each new adventure.

We drape the muted fabric of your Balinese sarong

over the satin lining of the coffin,

surround your stillness with mementos, smile,

weep, at shared stories of your well-lived,

well-loved life, strew petals on the strong

and perfect body that hid its fatal flaw

from you, from us.

Now it is time. We gather round this man,

the hub of all our lives. Hands joined, we sing,

speak final words. Leave with a last caress.

Now he is ready for this journey. We are not.

—Maude Meehan from *Washing the Stones*

~

intact. My mothering instinct was immediately there. I wasn't dressing a dead body, I was being my daughter's mother.

"That entire week and for sometime afterwards we were cushioned by shock with one foot in our own embodied world, one foot in the after world, what I came to call the 'between world.' The reality when you are in the between world is so different than what you and I imagine dealing with a dead body would be like. I felt absolutely connected to the experience of dressing her body.

"The utter absence of Melissa's spirit from her body was the first experience I had of her ongoing aliveness. What had animated her and made her so alive was so completely gone, yet I knew her spirit continued on somehow.

"We couldn't get her arms into the dress, so I cut her dress up the back and wrapped it around her. Her ears were already too stiff to put the earrings in. Her legs had been bandaged and taped because of the injuries, and there was no way that I was going to get stockings on her and her feet were so swollen I couldn't put her shoes on. One thing after another reminded us that she was dead.

"Yet there was a sense as we wove blue cornflowers into her hair that we were all being held in an ancient, completely known, kind of ritual. We were taking care of Melissa's body, preparing her for her journey. It was like dressing her for her wedding or the prom or for her first day of school. I felt I was wrapping her up to send her off to the next part of her journey, just like I unwrapped her when she was first born."

~

VANCE

"I feel if possible it's good to have the funeral at home," my friend Ann Hill told me. "It's the same way I feel about birth. It's the same kind of passage and carries a lot of the same kind of energy. My mother-in law, Vance, died in the hospital and her husband, Bill, was there with her as she died. He didn't know what to do next so they gave him a little sheet of paper that had a list of funeral homes and at the bottom of the list there was the Natural Death Care Project.

"Bill is a very frugal person so he decided to call the Natural Death Care people to see what they offered. They quoted him a price that was significantly lower then any of the funeral homes, so mostly out a sense of economics he decided, 'Well, this is fine.'

"I am glad he did. There was something about having the supplies—the dry ice, the blankets, the towels—everything all over the house. The smells. The washing of the body. You're constantly reminded of what is going on with this passage, the weight and the sense of this being in your home. It prepared me for the hole that was left behind when she died.

"We set up a little bed in our parlor and brought Vance in and laid her on a plastic sheet covered with towels. We took off her hospital gown and washed her body really well because the bacteria that's on the skin tends to make decomposition occur quicker. We used those blue ice freezer packs for the first day just to keep Vance cool and then the next morning we went out and got a bunch of dry ice. At first this process felt odd but then everybody actually really liked it. In fact it was hard trying to get the family to let go of her body by the end. They wanted to keep sitting with her to talk.

"Bill asked if I would officiate at the funeral and I said sure. I wanted to make the ceremony really inclusive because Vance and Bill's friends were a really mixed crowd, including: pagans, Episcopalians, and the woman who practices with the Miwok Indians down in Marin who did a purification ritual with bay leaves.

"The day of the funeral the priest told me what he planned to do. I told him I was officiating so he could tell me what he wanted to do and I would figure out when he could do it. It took him a little bit of time to realize that he wasn't actually in charge but he was very gracious about it.

"I opened with having everybody say their name and how they knew Vance. There were about forty people in the room. It was really wonderful hearing all these different parts of her life come together. We sang a wonderful song with words by Starhawk, set to the tune of *The Lily of the West*, called the *Island of the West*, and then my mom, who's a really great pianist, played *Silent Night* at the priest's request. People were in the mood for singing and Vance loved hearing everybody sing so that seemed appropriate. Her spirit was very strongly around. During the funeral when Father Ardley came up and said a few bracing verses of scripture and waved his little bell you could sense Vance's spirit going, 'Oh, okay, I've got my ticket here,' so off she went."

~

DOLORES

Melody LeBaron's mother was terminally ill and a friend from her church, who is a mortician and certified death educator, suggested to the family that they might like to prepare her body themselves. Melody discussed this idea with her sisters and their mother who was pleased for them to be the ones to dress her body for burial. Her three best friends also asked to be included.

Melody and her sisters laid out their mother's body with the help of these few close friends. Melody remembers this experience as the most intimate and profound in her life. "Because we had time to prepare for Mother's death, we had choices. The choice to make her death a natural, family experience was the beginning of our healing process. As a society, we support natural childbirth; at-home births are becoming common. We don't often think of death as a natural, at-home experience."

Even though she had time to mentally prepare for the experience, Melody was at first taken aback by the initial shock of being in the funeral home. "I don't remember if it was the strong antiseptic smell or the hard yellow light that I felt first. As the funeral director stepped back and I looked into the small bare room, I felt the cold penetrate my skin, going right to my heart. My mother's body was on the table naked under the sheet.

"We stood together looking at the still, cold form that had been my mother. But now touching her body didn't seem like a good idea at all. 'I can't do this,' I thought, panicking. I wanted to leave, to run out into the sunshine. I hesitated just inside the doorway, and I felt her presence as her words sounded clearly in my mind: 'You can do this, I will help you.' Her familiar mother love settled around me like a quilt.

"My sisters followed me into the room, anguish and uncertainty on their faces. 'She is here with us,' I told them. Gathering around the table, they too felt her nearness. I don't know how long we stood there, staring, each absorbed in her own thoughts and memories. Finally, remembering what we were there for, they turned to me for guidance. 'I'll do the makeup and then we'll dress the body,' I said. At the first hard, cold touch I drew back. Then the warmth and comfort I've felt so often before coursed through me. Somehow I knew what to do, how to cover the yellow skin with foundation and blush, how to select the proper eye shadow and lipstick colors. We carefully dressed her body, reminiscing quietly. We watched as our friend, Thelma, styled Mother's hair for the last time. I don't remember the exact words we spoke, only that the bonds of love between us grew strong. The room felt warm and sacred to me, as though I were participating in a holy ceremony.

"When we finished, we went to our father. Holding my hand, he walked up to the casket and looked inside. With tears of grief and gratitude, he hugged us and said, 'Thank you. You have made her look as beautiful as she always was.'"

Because their mother knew she was dying, Melody and her family had time to prepare. "She and my father had chosen the white, lacy dress she would be buried in. My mother and her 20 grandchildren were able to say honest and tender good-byes. My sisters and I had taken turns feeding her, washing her, rubbing her swelling feet, holding her hand as she dozed. I am grateful that it was my back that bent over her many photo albums, my hands that massaged her feet and washed and cared for her, our hearts that sang as we prepared her meals and fed her, our arms she died in, our love that compelled us to dress her body, our voices at her funeral, our eyes and ears that witnessed the love of her friends, our grief work begun."

Melody delivered the eulogy and the family, including the grandchildren, sang with the congregation. The graveside ceremony was short and they went back to the church for the reception where her mother had requested tables with photo albums and special mementos be set up. "We reminisced, ate, and laughed and talked while Handel's *Messiah* played and the children raced around the room," Melody remembers. "One by one friends said good-by, each with a special story about how Mother had touched their lives. Mother brought us into the world with love—we helped her leave with love."

CHAPTER SEVEN

It's Never Too Late
to Say Good-bye

If someone close to you dies before you've had a chance to make peace with them you can be left with a feeling of hopelessness and guilt. You may feel angry at yourself or at them for dying before you could reach out and heal old wounds, right wrongs, say you're sorry, or before they could tell you they were sorry. There can be many reasons why you may be left with guilt, unfinished business, full of regret. In a recent Gallup poll on death and dying 73 percent of people surveyed were worried that they might not have the chance to say good-bye to someone.

My friend Madeleine was left with unfinished business when her mother died. She was in her early twenties when her mother left the family to live in a religious community. As the years passed, her mother had less and less contact with her family until she finally cut herself completely off from them. Madeleine recalls: "Before she was with this group she was a Bahai, before that she was Jehovah's Witness, before that she was a Seventh Day Adventist, before that she was an Irish Catholic. She was looking for some more profound meaning in her life.

"I cared that she didn't communicate with us but I understood. There are a lot of religious groups that don't want you to communicate with family so that you can become free to follow your own spirit. I just can't understand why, when my mother knew she had breast cancer and was going to die, she never told us. She lied to her doctor and told him she had no family. We didn't even know when she died. We found out when my mother's lawyer notified us six weeks after she was buried.

"She left most of her belongings to people in her religious community. What hurts is that most family pictures and other memorabilia were lost. She was the caretaker of the family photos and I guess somebody in her community has them. Not having the photographs really matters to me. My mother spent the last ten to fifteen years of her life eight to ten hours a day writing on comparative religions and I would love to at least have seen her work. Mother just kind of disappeared. I am still very angry about my mother's death because there was no closure, no ceremony, no chance to say good-bye."

Ideally we would all live in a continual state of love and caring with every person in our lives. When someone important dies there would only be good memories and when we die we would be totally prepared and at peace with everyone. We would always be saying a conscious, loving hello until the final good-bye. Unfortunately, life isn't ideal so we have to figure out a way to experience closure and come to terms with unresolved loss if we are to live a healthy life.

Catherine has a stepdaughter who refuses to speak to her. She remains open and hopeful that her stepdaughter will change and is concerned that she might die before they resolve their differences. With everyone else in her life, Catherine tries to live as if she is always saying good-bye. Her philosophy is "To act like this is the last day of my life. What would I want to say to a person? I no longer hesitate to tell people I love them if I do. I am open and try not to carry unresolved issues around. We can die a lot more gracefully if we lead a, I won't say perfect, but an honest life."

If someone important to you dies and you are estranged, the unresolved grief can last indefinitely unless you do something about it. In order to begin the process of closure and forgiveness you must find a way to deal with the unfinished business no matter how many years have passed or how painful the experience.

I was recently a part of a Council of All Beings gathering. About twenty of us assembled on a ridge-top property overlooking the ocean for a spiritual ritual of healing and revival with the land and each other.

The process itself engendered respectful listening without judgement; speaking our truth without fear of criticism. Out of this process forgiveness seemed to naturally flow, and new beginnings seemed possible. For me as a participant two particular components were noteworthy; our agreement to set aside sacred time and to come together with intention. It brought forth the best in all of us and was extremely powerful.

Being part of this circle made me wish our culture had more rituals for forgiveness. It is so sad that we allow past transgressions, omissions, wrongs, hurtful words, and betrayals to follow us into the future, entangling our hearts, stifling our passion. How liberating it is to forgive, how healthy to ask forgiveness. I very much value the following words written by Jack Kornfield in his book *A Path With Heart:* "For most people forgiveness is a process. When you have been deeply wounded, the work of forgiveness can take years. It will go through many stages—grief, rage, sorrow, fear, and confusion—and in the end, if you let yourself feel the pain you carry, it will come as a relief, as a release for your heart. You will see that forgiveness is fundamentally for your own sake, a way to carry the pain of the past no longer."

There are two sides to forgiveness—whether you have wounded or been wounded, it's the healing that matters. In the Jewish tradition of Yom Kippur, ten days are set aside for you to look in your heart and see if you have hurt anyone, and, if so, go to them and apologize. One hopes that they will forgive you and often just the gesture of your asking may be all it takes. An important part of the 12-step process of Alcoholics Anonymous is to identify people you have harmed and ask their forgiveness.

If you find yourself with a negative outlook on life or a compromised immune system, look within and see if you have some forgiving to do. Even if you have been wounded, it may still be necessary to make the first overture. Sometimes the best thing to do is leave an opening and invite the other person in. If you are harmed and the other person has no intention of working through the situation with you, if they deny you the opportunity, you may have to do it by yourself through meditation, counseling, art, music, writing, or horticultural therapy—whatever works for you. Instead of fuming in a dark hole, paint, sing, or garden yourself to forgiveness and health. Forgiveness is like love, it is best given uncon-ditionally, with no expectations on the side of the forgiver. Often the per-son who needs to be forgiven first is you. This wisdom can heal the deepest wounds.

When my daughter, Sasha Harrison, finished one of her paintings she felt transformed. After she showed me the painting I asked her to write how it felt to let go of her anger.

"This painting saved me after thirty years of deep sadness. I carried around a heavy heart. At the age of eight I was introduced to racism at a public school in a rural set-ting. I was taunted and teased regularly, called names and laughed at. That was basi-cally my school experience until I got my GED at fifteen. When I looked back on those years I would feel intense pain deep in my bones.

"I sat down to paint and the girl appeared. She seemed to need advice so I painted the Elder Woman. I added the Indian because it felt important to do so. When I was fin-ished I knew what it meant. My ancestors, the Indian and African women were asking me to forgive my Caucasian ancestor's children (represented by the shapes at the top of the painting), open my heart, and let them back in the way it was meant to be.

"Now when I look back at my school years I feel none of the pain and none of the sor-row and none of the shame. Only forgiveness."

I had an important conversation over brunch one Sunday with my friend Carter Smith, a very talented and successful clothing designer. Carter's parents died within a week of each other and their passing had a major impact on his life. Clearly losing both his parents so close to one another caused him to go deep within and to allow the preciousness of life to bubble up and remain close to the surface. As we prepare to go our separate ways, he gave me a gem that I carry with me and bring out at least once a day. He said "Love is for giving; Love is forgiving."

Grief is not something you just "get over," but with a good support system and the passage of time almost everyone is able to adjust to the loss and go forth with their lives. If you have unresolved issues or didn't get to mourn in a way that was meaningful to you, you probably feel stuck, unable to move forward. It might seem like it's too late. But I promise you, no matter how many years have passed it is *not too late to forgive, not too late to say good-bye.* You can still forgive and even if the person has died you can still be forgiven, and you can always forgive yourself. I believe the choice is yours. Anger takes a part of your life away. With work you can release your anger and get that part of your life back. In his book *A Year to Live, How to Live This Year as if It Were Your Last*, Stephen Levine tells us, "Certainly one need never stop speaking with the departed just because their body and heart have returned to their respective sources. The heart is the bridge across which we can encourage them to follow their deepest healing, to forgive and allow themselves to be forgiven, to enter the light of their great nature."

Sue Brown, a psychotherapist in Santa Rosa, California, works with many people in her practice that have experienced death without closure. "I'm convinced," she says, "that what's really difficult is that we have a sense of an ongoing relationship with someone who has died but we are confused because there is no body to relate to anymore. That lack of embodiment is the most difficult part of a death because the spiritual traditions that we grow up with or the spiritual traditions we are developing don't feel very embodied or satisfying.

"With my mom's death and my daughter, Melissa's, death I really understood why people construct a heaven, because it makes an image, a place, a way to relate to people. I understand why people go to gravesites and talk to their loved one. They know they are not physically there but they are trying to get connected with the ongoing relationship. We mistakenly identify letting go of the relationship with the completion of the grieving.

"I believe the relationship transforms and changes and we gradually let go of the investment we have in the relationship as it existed here. I think the best description of successful mourning is that our energy gets gradually freed up to invest in other relationships and creative projects, other kinds of life."

In the process of writing this book I realized I had not experienced closure with the death of my father. My father and I had a very close relationship for the first years of my life. Then suddenly he was taken ill and we had to sell our home in Florida and move to Ohio where he was hospitalized. I missed the sunshine, the ocean, the happy times, and most of all my father. My dad never came back to me. We lived far away from the hospital and mom and I were only able to visit him once a week. Our bond still remained strong until I moved to San Francisco at the age of nineteen. In those days midwesterners didn't often leave home, especially young women, and I became somewhat of a black sheep in my family. Except for occasional visits and letters, my relationship with Dad was frozen in time, based primarily on memories.

When my father died of heart failure in a hospital in Ohio, I was not invited to his funeral. My mother told me there was no need to come home. I was a flower child in the Haight-Ashbury counterculture, a single mom with a small child of my own. I had no money and no one offered to send me a ticket. I was not there to grieve with everyone else. I heard later that the church overflowed with people who loved my father, but I missed the funeral of the man who gave me life and whose death I am just beginning to mourn. I didn't understand at the time why it was so important to grieve with others. My dad went to heaven in Cincinnati and that was that.

I can't change the past. But I can deal with it now instead of sweeping the hurt aside. In the past when I thought of my father a huge lump of sadness would form in my throat. I was dwelling in the land of unresolved grief and doing nothing about it. Now when I think of my father I remember the good times we had together and all he taught me. I have rekindled our relationship. I have forgiven my father for enlisting in the war as a teenager and becoming a war hero, thus robbing me of the healthy father I longed for while I was growing up. I have forgiven my relatives who were unable to realize the extent of my need for him. I have forgiven myself for not being stronger and going to his funeral. I have not yet forgiven a society that would sacrifice its youth to war and I may never be able to. I am doing the best I can. Part of forgiveness is recognizing and accepting that we are all doing the best we can.

My father passed on his love of gardening to me and I treasure the memories of being three and four and helping him with the tomatoes and flowers he planted in a circle in our front yard. It was so like him to create a playful, unique garden. The Coffin Garden discussed in Chapter 5 is the place I go to reflect and communicate with my father. I built an altar there in his honor that has an opening in the center to symbolize our ongoing relationship.

Last week the women in the Threshold Choir, of which I am a member, sang a song to help me dedicate the garden. As we sang I said a private good-bye to my father so he can feel free to go on with the rest of his evolution and I with mine.

Dorothy lost her husband, Bernard, to dementia after a ten-year illness. She thought she had said good-bye to her husband and made the adjustment to his being gone from her life. However, a year after his death she realized that while she mourned the man who had been ill she had not mourned the man she had loved.

"I live my life differently because of having loved Bernard and being loved by him," Dorothy told me one morning as we sat together in her living room. "That's the most significant change in my life. That's stronger than the experience of losing him. I cried so much during all of the years that Bernard was ill that I felt I had already done a lot of my grieving. And that's what the books all said, too, so I said, 'Well, that must be right then.'

"Also I was extraordinarily relieved when he died, that he was not going to starve to death in front of my eyes, that he died very quickly. I wasn't going to have to watch him gasp for every breath with pneumonia or something. When he stopped breathing I was tremendously relieved. Probably more for me than for him.

"I no longer had to think about when I had to be home … how late I could stay away … scheduling things. It had become increasingly difficult for me to care for Bernard even for short periods of time. I just found it harder and harder to do. I think I was worn out.

"I spent the first six months grieving some, crying some, but it seems like the second six months was harder because memories of the former Bernard and our relationship before he got sick, came back. So I'm now grieving for the man that I fell in love with. When I'm with people I generally feel pretty good. I feel the grief when I'm sitting here by myself just thinking about Bernard.

"My stepson, Andy, did a wonderful thing. When I first met Bernard he had one of those old reel-to-reel tape recorders and he taped everything. Our first Christmas with the kids—everything. Andy went through all those reel-to-reel tapes and made a tape that includes a letter Bernard wrote to me when I had gone back to Minnesota the year after we met. There was also a letter from my mother to me and a letter from myself to my mother. There was an excerpt of Bernard reading something in German... German has all those funny vowels and consonants and he reads this and just has a fit of laughter—falls on his butt laughing!

"I find it very comforting listening to these tapes. When I'm in the middle of my grief I love to listen to his voice. I begin to remember him more clearly. I can either listen to funny parts or I can play the letter where he tells me how empty the house is without me and how much he misses and loves me, which is very lovely to hear."

Some spirits are easy to send on their way; others like Bernard's linger on. Dorothy had lived so long with the stress and strain of taking care of her husband that she had no time to come to terms with her husband's dementia; she was too busy living it. When he died she could say good-bye to the sick Bernard but still needs time to grieve for the incredibly ebullient man she had married. Fortunately she understands this and trusts her own wisdom.

It is part of grief to remember.
Ovid

Ina created a very courageous and healing ritual for herself. Her mother was diagnosed with a brain tumor when Ina was five years old and died when Ina was fifteen. Even though her mother had been dead for thirty-five years, every time during the part of the Jewish service when the congregation would remember those who had died during the past year, an intense sadness would wash over Ina. The death of her mother was an open wound that would not heal. It is traditional to light a Yartzheit candle on the anniversary of a loved one's death so Ina decided on the anniversary of her mother's death she would hold a public ceremony at her temple. She sent out invitations and asked people to bring round breads or pies—any food that would express the wholeness of life in the form of a circle. At the ceremony the rabbi, her friends, and the congregation gathered around Ina to help her bury her mother once and for all.

Carole is a waitress in a seaside hotel where I stayed for several days. She knew I was writing this book and one evening she left a note by my plate, asking if I would talk with her. It was late at night in the kitchen when she poured out her story to me.

When Carole was fifteen she was raped and became pregnant. She had a little boy that she gave up for adoption to a family who could care for him, as she could not. She went on with her life and had two daughters, both now grown, who, over the years urged her to find their lost brother. She was reluctant to disrupt her son's life. When Carole would daydream about her son she could never see him as any more than an infant. For these reasons she refused to try and contact him. Recently Carole's daughters called to tell her they had located the adoptive parents and that their brother had died at two months of age.

Tears filled her eyes as Carole told her painful story. Her friends did not understand her grief and were not very supportive. They felt that because she never knew her son, and it was such a long time ago, how could she possibly have these feelings. But Carole does have feelings of guilt and sadness. She now knows for certain that her son is dead and needs to acknowledge the pain she is feeling and to forgive herself. She must begin to mourn now, 36 years later.

Yom Kippur is the time of year when Jews bring to mind the memories of their deceased relatives. Rabbi David A. Cooper, a leader of the Jewish Reconstructionist Movement, lecturer, scholar, and noted author of *God Is a Verb*, usually guides his congregation in a powerful visualization which he says, "Brings a flood of tears and a great deal of healing."

If someone close to you died that you didn't get to say a proper good-bye to I recommend adapting his visualization to your own situation. I was so impressed with Rabbi Cooper's method that I have included (with his blessings) his entire visualization exercise.

Rabbi Cooper advises that before you begin, if there is a censor within you that inhibits you about this exercise, let yourself experience it anyway. He further cautions that you not begin this practice with anyone who has brought you great violence or severe abuse.

1. Find a protected, quiet place where you will not be disturbed for about thirty minutes. Sit in a comfortable position, close your eyes, and let your attention rest on bodily sensations.

2. After a few minutes of relaxation, allow the images of dear ones who have died come into your mind. Notice how you feel as these images arise.

3. Pick only one to work with. Let this image rest in your mind. Try to communicate with it telepathically, or even using an imaginary voice inside your mind. Ask the image anything you wish. Some questions might be:

∿ What is it like where you are?

∿ What was it like when you first died?

∿ Who else is there with you?

∿ Have you visited anyone living in their dreams?

4. Now, ask the image: "Tell me the things that you feel you did well while you were alive. What are the things that you are proud of having done?" (Let it speak to you.)

5. Next, ask: "And what are the things that you feel you did not do so well in your lifetime? What are the things you regret the most?" (Let it speak. You may find yourself getting sad at this point. Try to stay connected as best you can.)

6. Then ask: "If you could choose one thing that you regret the most, what would it be? If you could live your life over, what would be the most important thing you would change?"

7. Now, allow the image to fade into the background. Try to remember a situation that actually occurred with this person when they were alive. *You want to bring this event into your imagination as if your deceased partner were living her life over again.* Your task is to remember this event as if it occurred the way they would have wanted so that they would not have regrets. See the event anew, in its more perfect form. Let yourself replay it in this new way over and over again for a few minutes.

8. Let go of the event and invite the image back into your mind. Notice how you are feeling. Ask it, "Is this the way you would like to be remembered?" If it says yes, agree to try to build up these memories. If it says no, find out what it would like, and try to do it that way the next time.

9. Promise to return and ask if it will come back again. Hopefully, the image will agree to do so. Bid farewell for now, and give it a hug if you can. Take a couple of deep breaths and open your eyes.

Once you have identified a particular attribute to work on for some- one who has died, allow yourself to meditate regularly on the person, always imagining situations in a way that idealizes how this person would have acted if they had the chance to do it over again. This is what heals the dead because it begins to change and softens your feelings toward this person.

Rabbi Cooper says: "The key to this practice is obviously the reframing of our memories. If we want to hold on to old and painful memories because 'that is the way it was,' we remain stuck, as does the one with whom we are working. If we can use our imagination to re-create our memories, we begin to free ourselves and thereby release sparks for the souls of the dead.

"This is not a practice of denial. It is a practice of forgiving and regenerating. Everyone enters this life with a pure soul. We are stuck with our fate, the work we have to do, and our intrinsic strengths and weaknesses. We often make a mess on one level or another. Just as we hope we will be forgiven, we need to find a way to forgive others. Each time we are able to do so, the universe is raised one more notch in its consciousness."

Forgiveness makes a lot of sense once you realize how much continual damage you do to yourself by reliving the negative emotions of a distasteful event over and over again. Forgiveness is a practice that heals both your psyche and your immune system.

The following story illustrates how harmful unresolved grief can be and how freeing it is to forgive. It took Bronwyn years to come to terms with the death of both of her parents until she was finally able to say good-bye in an unusual case of spontaneous healing. "Shortly after my mother's death," she remembers, "I was living away from home and working as a waitress. I started having dreams about my mother, that her body was chopped up in a garbage bag and all kinds of awful things. I had never had very pleasant dreams about her or a pleasant relationship with her but these dreams were horrible. I remember feeling at the time, 'Oh my God, what is happening to me!'

"Because I didn't know what a severe depression was before I started having these dreams, or how to deal with it, I just stayed depressed for a very long time. After two years, I came out of my depression and started to grieve for my mother and I felt horror and pity for the terrible life that she had. I felt horror and pity for the fact that we had not been able to know each other.

"Eleven days after my mother died my alcoholic father had the first of thirteen heart attacks in the space of ten years. This first heart attack nearly killed him. I lived those ten years in constant fear I would get a phone call in the middle of the night telling me he had died. My mother's death was a complete shock; my father's was a relief. I remember him looking up at me saying, 'Why don't I just go?' He was angry at the fact that his body hadn't let him go.

"Many years after my parents died I had an interesting experience. I had hurt my back and was working with a very good massage therapist. She worked on me for about an hour and then left me in a darkened room. Suddenly I felt my parents' presence with me in the room. I held their hands and we talked. I told them all of the things that I missed about them; all of the things I loved about them and how sorry I felt about their lives. We talked and talked, and I cried and then we said good-bye. It was spontaneous and came out of the void. I didn't call for them.

There was no conscious effort on my part ... they just showed up and they left.

"Those bad dreams about my mother vanished. Once in awhile I dream about both of my parents but they are always friendly dreams. Whenever they come to me in my sleep I know that they are with me and they are trying to tell me something as if they are my spirit guides, or they are just saying, 'Hi kid, how are you doing?' They had violent lives and horrible deaths but I feel they are now at peace, and I am much more at peace with them."

No matter what the circumstances it's never too late to say good-bye, never too late to forgive yourself and others. The old adage, "better late than never" is an understatement when dealing with unresolved feelings about someone who has died.

CHAPTER EIGHT

Turning Fear into Passion

At some point in our lives, we realize we are mortal. This realization, that death is not optional, is part of what makes us human. To learn to accept the inevitability is one of the biggest challenges of living. Feeling vulnerable can be frightening, but it can also be liberating. Use this understanding and choose to live with more gusto, to push beyond boundaries and to invite passion in. By learning to live side by side with death and being aware that we don't know how much time we have left, we can have a more ecstatic life. How we live life determines how we die.

Creating passion in your life is probably the best gift you will ever give yourself. Passion is the rocket fuel for aliveness. It is a driving force and an inspiration. Passion for life can take the sting out of death because passion helps keep our loved ones alive within us. Passion is infectious and motivating. It inspires you to jump lightly from your bed in the morning and to lie down at night with a feeling of fullness.

Nothing dims passion faster than fear. We live in a fear-based culture, where we learn at a young age to avoid risk, to protect and shield ourselves from life in order to feel 'safe.' So invasive is this fear that it has caused us to become alienated from our common humanity and has diluted our sacred connections with one another both living and dead. As Kathleen Dowling Singh notes in her moving book, *The Grace in Dying,* "For most people who are dying in America, there is a lack of spiritual context. Dying is frightening in every conceivable way. The extinction, even temporarily, of the internal dialogue for one who is dying and may never have practiced a spiritual discipline could be described as a 'black hole' in psychic space."

In this society, the ultimate fear is the fear of death. This fear can infiltrate your entire being, trample your spirit, and rob you of your joy and passion. Fear of death is especially painful because we do not acknowledge it. Death is so taboo, so mysterious, so outside our day-to-day lives, that we act as if it isn't part of the life cycle. Because death isn't included in our life equation, we don't like to speak of it unless we have to, and then only in hushed tones.

Miriam Redstone is one of the most insightful people I know and I have been fortunate to walk with her most Saturday mornings for years. We have laughed and cried together and shared the many ups and downs of life including the death of both her father and mother. On one foggy Saturday walk she told me, "I have much less fear since being present at the death of my dad. I think it comes from the joy at the moment, the after death glow. It was so unexpected. I experienced my dad working during the last week of his life. I saw him go back in time and looking really young. I saw his body change from being a very young man to getting older and older and older until he died. Some of the family were so afraid they wouldn't even go in the room—to me it was a high point in my life."

We all know what the "flight or fight" kind of fear feels like—clammy hands, a racing heart, holding your breath, adrenaline raging around your body. But what about the subtler kind of fear that cuts you off from the good stuff by making you feel like your feet are stuck in glue because you are too timid to take a risk, the kind of fear that freezes your heart and seizes your mind.

The flight or fight kind of fear protects you in times of danger, but the fear of taking risks does no good at all. It's usually an imagined fear, the fear of 'what if' which saps your energy. An imagined fear is rarely as bad as you imagine it. Imagined fear is really fear of life, which slams doors on opportunity, steals your health and your joy, and starves your soul.

Lisa's father was in the process of dying, and his fear of death seemed to occupy most of his waking hours. His wife and daughter wanted to give him peace of mind, and they came up with a daily process that was soothing for him and the whole family. Each morning they played some beautiful music and led him on a guided visual voyage through a warm glowing tunnel of light where the Virgin Mary (his idea of what the ideal death was about) would welcome him with open arms and a smiling face. This daily practice set the emotional tone for his remaining weeks. His fears were eased and changed by the daily practice of transcendental passion and love. His family was with him when he died, and they all felt at peace when, with his final breath, he smiled and extended his arms upward.

You don't have to wait until death is imminent to turn fear into passion—you can begin today to create a blueprint to feel more alive. In his groundbreaking book, *How We Die*, Sherwin Nuland notes, "The dignity that we seek in dying must be found in the dignity with which we have lived our lives. *Ars moriendi* is *ars vivendi*: The art of dying is the art of living. The honesty and grace of the years of life that are ending is the real measure of how we die. It is not in the last weeks or days that we compose the message that will be remembered, but in all the decades that preceded them."

Learning to Risk

More than any other factor, the willingness to risk will determine your ability to find passion. It is through taking risks that you can practice pushing beyond your greatest expectations and surpassing your hopes and dreams.

Risk can be about things like bungee jumping or spelunking, but primarily it means switching the button in your head that says "No, I can't" to "Yes, I can." The power of changing your attitude to embrace change cannot be overstated. When you change your attitude, seemingly insurmountable obstacles can be mastered and you begin to take charge of your life.

My sister, Jean, who raised five children and is a grandmother of eleven, decided to take a risk and by doing so overcame her fear of performing and greatly enriched her life. "I was pressured and persuaded by a number of the players in our dulcimer society to go out and play in public. It took all the nerve I had, plus not being able to eat beforehand. I was scared to death the first time I did it. After that it was easy because I really loved the instrument. I eventually learned to love performing. I met so many wonderful people. My passion overcame my fear. I find that now it's so much easier to express myself. I can talk to anyone and not be nervous about it. It is so rewarding to feel that with my playing, I can bring joy and happiness to many people. I've made so many more new friends, really good friends. From taking the risk came much happiness. Not that I wasn't happy before—but it is a different type of happiness.

"My husband and I have been married over fifty years and he told me recently, 'I can't believe how performing has changed your life!"

Coming to terms with death is a process. You can start overcoming smaller fears by taking risks. You can challenge yourself, as Jean did, and take on something that makes you feel 'scared to death.' Whether it be skydiving or speaking out about someone cutting down your favorite tree before the town council, taking a risk is almost always exhilarating. Every risk you take makes you stronger. Every risk you take puts you more in charge of your life. Soon you will be experiencing your life as an adventure instead of a field of landmines that have to be navigated.

One secret to mastering the art of risk taking is to take on smaller challenges first before you attempt a major one. Make it the smallest risk you can take and still feel that you have been challenged. From success with small risks comes confidence. The strategy I have found that works best is to break things into small increments and conquer your fear a little at a time. Be sure to acknowledge the tiniest of baby steps. Just as real babies flourish through appreciation, so will you. Self-acknowledgement will turn your baby steps into confident strides.

In addition to fearing what others think, you must also battle the cultural bias against risk. Risk involves both mistakes and successes. We learn very early that it's not okay to make mistakes; that right answers are good and incorrect answers are bad. You've probably learned, along with the rest of us, to keep your mistakes to a minimum by resisting change and avoiding risk.

Anytime we try something new, we risk failure and chaos. Unfortunately, this stops us from enjoying valuable learning and living experiences. *The problem is, most people consider success and failure as opposites, not as products of the same process.* Prior to the industrial revolution, the word "success" meant journey or progress toward a goal. It was not a destination. If you see your life more as a journey than a series of successes and failures, then you remove the judgment from an event and free yourself to move ahead without fear. An experience or event only becomes a failure if you decide it is a failure.

Overcoming fear and learning to risk is fundamental to creating passion in your life. Break the risk into small parts, and don't move on until you have conquered each part. The secret is to trust in yourself and to take one step at a time.

I see fear as the small dark room you go into to change your clothes before you dive and swim. It's cramped and smells damp and there are small voices talking in your head saying, "Don't go out there and dive into that dangerous ocean." You have to make a conscious decision while in that uncomfortable place to open the door and change your reality, recreating your life's plan. I love what Georgia O'Keefe has to say about fear and have taped her words on the door to my office so I see them every day. She writes, "I have been absolutely terrified every day of my life but I have never let that keep me from doing anything I wanted to do."

My husband and I were building our dream house on twenty wilderness acres in California when I contracted Lyme disease. After putting all of our money and four years of our lives into creating our home, we had to leave it because I was too ill to live in such a remote place. We moved into town.

I felt completely blindsided by this diagnosis. I felt defeated and hopeless and unable to see any light ahead. Finally I realized that I had to gradually expand my vision to allow more light into my mind to help me to lift my body and spirit out of bed. I made a list of my most important missions in life and vowed that if I was allowed to live, I would pursue only these dreams. My first mission was to paint in France. I began to live the vision by cutting and pasting photos in my journal about painting in fields of sunflowers. I wrote pages of plans about buying a small house in France and creating a haven for my friends and myself to live our dreams in. Creating a new dream and taking the baby steps to make it happen opened the door to treasures and riches of the heart that I could not have imagined.

My husband and I took a vacation in France, and some of my women friends pitched in with loans of money and physical labor to help me buy and refurbish an old medieval house in a small village. In order to repay them and connect with a new life, I started giving painting workshop/vacations during the summers. During the first workshop I was still so sick that I could only stand up and paint for a half an hour at a time. Afterwards I would lay in the car for an hour to regain my strength. I got a hat with a turtle on it and began to practice accepting the idea that my new life was going to be in "turtle mode." I wrote power words across my canvas before beginning each painting. For example, "She knew the French light would make her well," and "Dive and swim and don't look back."

Now, six years after my near-death experience, I have a totally different life with a thriving business called Global Live Art, where I teach painting and the principals of living your life as an art form. The smaller house in town where we now live offers us the freedom to travel and do creative work, which wouldn't have been so easy in our 'dream house' in the country. I am thankful for the trauma that helped me wake up and take a different road where I now concentrate on healing, vitality, and expression on a daily basis.

Of course, everyone will approach death's prompting and reinvent their lives in their own way. For people who write as a way to tap into the parts of them that would otherwise remain invisible, it's important to set aside daily time and to write until the new visions and plans evolve. As Julia Cameron notes in her *The Right to Write*, "Writing is alchemy. Writing that poem, moving out of the cramped and cerebral space of bitterness into the capacious heart, I am no longer a victim, an enemy, an injured party. I am what I am again: a writer. I have metabolized the injury into art."

Visual people will need to see what the next phase could look like by playing with collage, searching out nurturing environments, imagining a reality that will lift the spirit and challenge new insights for major change to ensue.

For logical, analytical people, it helps to learn to quiet the mind and get beyond the conditioned sense of self that they have accepted as home. Eventually the point will come when you have looked at everything from all perspectives and the only answer will be to let go of your mind. After engaging in transcendental and Zen meditation, I found that Vipassana meditation (where you engage in ten days of silence and in-depth learning) is a process that works for me and others I know, especially those who believe there is no hope.

In a vital life, one never reaches a place where it makes sense to quit searching. Searching can initiate the beginning of change. We can let the small and large deaths of patterns, relationships, and the people we love lead us to a more satisfying quality of life.

Creativity lifts you beyond your resistance, over the edge of fear, and onto the wild ride of new possibilities. Change and commitment to your new options can lead to profound personal growth. Creativity, growth, chaos, and death are the continual cycle necessary for turning fear into passion.

As part of learning to live with death at my side and to create more aliveness, I made the commitment to be open to suggestions from friends and people I meet on my path. Because I usually say yes, even when I am afraid—*especially* when I am afraid—I have been blessed with many gifts.

Rejoicing in the Shadow

The shadow side is the wellspring of creativity where all that is unique about you awaits release. The shadow is that part of yourself you don't understand, the chaos that sometimes terrifies you—the out of control, loose, dangerous, no rules part. The shadow is all of the shame, lust, rage, greed, and violent traits that you try and hide from yourself as well as others. But turning away from your shadow side drains your precious energy. In *A Little Book on the Human Shadow,* Robert Bly describes the shadow side as "the long bag we drag behind us." The bigger the bag, according to Bly, the less energy one has. Passion, on the other hand, gives you an abundance of energy.

In our Global Live Art workshops we include many opportunities for self-expression with the focus on art and journaling. We encourage you to use both as conduits to the spiritual. By tapping into your creativity the gifts you were born to give to the world spring forth. Creativity is healing to the soul and makes life visible, shining a light into the dark side so you can know what cannot be accessed in any other way. It allows you to tap into the mysterious. Creativity ignites passion.

Tamara Slayton, the founder of the Initiative for the Renewal of Modern Culture, believes that "Art is a universal access point and can help prepare us for an integrated death." Tamara has created an exercise that she uses in her workshops to encourage participants to draw their personal picture of what they imagine death is about so they can open a door into a new understanding. "When someone draws their picture of death they get a snapshot, a focus, of where they are right now, and then something is revealed about where they might like to be. Artistic activities are the medicines for helping us bridge the dimensions between living and dying. Every time you pick up a paintbrush you go through a microcosm of dying and being reborn. The soul is able to knit together disparate qualities—paint, brush, paper, fear—

and then interweave those disparate experiences together into some-thing beautiful."

Every artist knows that without the deep purple and black shadows the painting will look flat and lack dimension. If you don't include, and benefit from, the shadow in your life, you may find yourself with a pretty unexciting life-canvas. If you stay stuck in grays and neutrals too long your spirit withers. As the artist Carol Golden notes, "You have to allow for the river of darkness in every painting."

Your shadow side still exists, whether you acknowledge it or not, and when ignored it can sneak up on you in the form of illness, depression, isolation, and apathy. Apathy is a Greek word that means "unsuffering." Apathy means you can't or don't want to experience pain, so you shut down, pull in your energy, and your light dims and eventually goes out.

The homeopath Randy Shelly says, "You just think healing is about going towards the light and it's not. You've got to embrace your whole self. You've got to know which parts of you are your power sources. We are all born with a vital force—if it's not flowing then we are less than we could be. If you keep flowing, you get to experience more. If you get stuck, you lose yourself. Your dark side is just as much your power source as your light side."

I am finally beginning to meet my shadow side. I used to think that if I was open to the shadow I would be pulled bit by bit into a black murky lagoon. Monsters would jump out through the murk, grab me by the throat, and pull me under. Glub, glub. But the opposite is true. I have

Meditation

I have been raised on a diet of fear. Let me dine instead at the table of possibility. I have been taught to devalue and diminish myself. Let me aim now to honor my true gifts. I have neglected to mark important passages, to acknowledge myself. Let me begin now to celebrate the first steps of change, and to congratulate myself often. Let me rejoice in the life cycle and honor the natural ways. Let me accept life as it is. Let me remember to love my dreams, as they can come true.

learned that by repressing the negative, I give up my power. I know that the shadow is a valuable ally, the key to untapped potential.

Accessing the shadow side can be tricky, but full of riches. Listed in the bibliography are several fascinating books and there are many Jungian psychologists specifically trained in helping you to get in touch with your shadow. There is also art and journaling practice. Whatever method you choose, making the commitment to access the unknown is the important first step. For those of you who have ignored or repressed your dark side, I encourage you to at least be open to the potential power that can occur when you embrace all of you. In *The Undiscovered*

Self, Carl Jung tells us that the dark side is 90 percent gold, and that by embracing our dark side we can become whole.

The Art of Dying is about learning to write a good story for your life, about saying hello to passion and good-bye to fear. By turning fear of death into passion for life, you can help change the culture and create a more loving, compassionate, peaceful world. Mozart put it beautifully, "Death is the true and best friend of humanity, the key which unlocks the door to our true state of happiness."

Steps to Creating
a Memorial Ritual

By Jill Goffstein

Rituals can be simple or elaborate, structured or informal, depending on what best reflects the life of the diseased. They can be approached in many different ways depending on whether there are any important religious affiliations, what you are or are not comfortable with, and the size and location of the gathering.

If you are in charge of the ceremony, one way to involve those closest to the person who died and to create a meaningful tribute is by meeting together as soon as possible. At this planning meeting, you might set up an impromptu altar of photos, candles, and flowers to help stimulate memories of joyful, funny, and sweet times and to give a physical focus to the gathering. The stories and anecdotes that emerge will help in the creation of a ritual that reflects the character and values of your loved one. This time together will also create a strong support for the days ahead.

It is important to have an underlying structure even if the memorial or funeral service is an informal gathering. A traditional service would include an opening prayer, the singing of hymns, readings, a eulogy by the one conducting the service or a close family member, and a closing prayer. If it is informal you can use the "Stages of a Ritual" on page 177 for options to personalize the ceremony.

Some questions that can help you design the service are: How would this person want to be remembered—for the buildings she designed as an architect, for his work with troubled youth, for her beautiful embroidery, for his kindness to others? What have you learned from her? What were his special gifts and talents? If she was a poet, read her favorite poems. If he was a jazz musician, have a jam session as part of the ceremony or play his favorite music. What are the stories that are told about her? What was particularly unique about this person?

There is no right or wrong way to honor your loved one. Use your imagination and be guided by your heart and the respect you feel for this individual.

Choose a family member or a close friend to conduct the memorial or you may choose to do this yourself. This person should be someone who is not emotionally devastated by the loss and is comfortable leading a group and speaking in public. The role of this person is to open and close the ceremony, introduce speakers, and invite guests to participate. Choose carefully because he or she will set the tone of the ritual.

Often a eulogy is given and becomes a central focus of the ceremony, as it expresses the essence of the life of the person who died and how he or she touched the lives of others. Sometimes it's appropriate for several people from different facets of the person's life to speak. It's a good idea to give them some time parameters to keep things flowing.

The whole ceremony should be a comfortable length of time, neither too long nor too short. If there are too many speakers, people get restless and uncomfortable. However, if the ritual is too short, the mourners may feel rushed and incomplete. An hour to an hour and a half is the right length of time.

When creating a ritual, think of the ways people can participate. The involvement of the guests deepens the experience of all those present. In the following section, you will find examples of ways to elicit participation from those who attend the ritual.

Once you know what will be included in the ceremony you can prepare a program. It can be as simple as a single sheet of pretty paper folded in half, or as formal as a printed and engraved booklet. It is helpful for people to know what to expect and serves as a keepsake not only for the family but also for everyone who attends. Traditionally, on the front of the program the person's name is printed with the years of life and death. Often there is a favorite photo. Inside the program list the order of events of the ceremony, including the names of the speakers, and musical selections or the names of the live musicians, if applicable. You can also include inspirational poems or prayers and the words of any songs that will be sung. This is also a good place to extend an invitation to the reception afterwards (with directions, if necessary).

Make a list of all of the details. Some of the logistics to keep in mind are: parking, seating, podium for speaker (if needed), programs, flowers, arranging of flowers, candles, other items for the altar, a sound system, written directions to the reception, if necessary. Also ask yourself the following questions: Who will be the greeters? What arrangements can be made if it rains? Where will coats be hung? Who will keep track of the gifts of flowers or donations to a designated charity? Will you want to be either audiotaping or videotaping the ceremony? Will the ritual and reception be at the same location? What will be served at the reception? There are always friends who come forward and ask how they can help. With this list, you can offer them a way to make a contribution and spread out the work as well.

After years of doing rituals, I found that there are basic components to a ceremony. These work for any rights of passage and I've adapted these stages for the memorial ritual. You may find it helpful to use the format below to structure your service. These are not rules . . . just suggestions to get you started. Feel free to let your heart and imagination lead to your own creation.

Stages of a Ritual:

~ Preparing the Ritual Space

~ Greeting

~ Grounding and Centering

~ Creating a Sacred Space

~ Sharing/Heart Connection

~ Sending Blessings/Letting Go

~ Closing

Preparing the Ritual Space: Create an altar on a table, fireplace mantle, or other central spot. An altar is an important place to honor the life force of the your loved one. Fill it with flowers, votive candles, and especially photos of the person at different stages of his or her life. Add personal belongings that symbolize the individual being honored: something she made with her own hands, a hat he always wore, or her favorite book. If she always gave silver dollars to her nieces and nephews, put a bowl of silver dollars on the altar. If he was a ceramist, include some of his clay pots. If she was a fabulous baker, have a dish of her famous cookies. Or, if he collected heart-shaped rocks, scatter them on the altar. Use whatever feels authentic and conjures up what was special about the person you are honoring.

Decorate the gathering place with flowers or plants and set up a table for the food after the ceremony, if the reception is to be held at the same location as the ritual. Set the chairs in a circle, semicircle, or in rows and do not forget to have aisles so people can get to their seats easily. Save a central section for the immediate family by taping a long ribbon across the chairs. If you are not using chairs for everyone, be sure to have some available for those who can't stand for long periods.

Traditionally, a guest register is placed near the entrance to the ceremony for guests to sign so the family can have a record of those who were present. You can also be creative and offer other ways for people to record their presence. One idea is to have guests write their names and a message on light-colored cloth squares with fabric pens. These can be sewn together after the ceremony and made into a wall hanging, quilt cover, or cloth book for the family. Another possibility is to have the attendees sign a beveled mirror table runner using a diamond-tipped pen. This mirror can then become the centerpiece of a memorial table or altar at the family's home.

If the ceremony involves the planting of a tree or flowers, the guests could paint their names on medium-sized river rocks that can be purchased at a landscaping supply store. These rocks of friendship are used to encircle the tree or edge a flower garden planted in the memory of the person who died. When all the rocks are placed, it is quite moving. Use an acrylic paint for easy clean up of brushes and spills. After the ceremony, coat the names with UV sealer to protect them from the weather.

For sweet, heartfelt group involvement, you may choose to have paper origami boats or paper hearts available for people to write messages to the deceased or their family. Someone might volunteer to string them together for a keepsake.

An unusual and powerful event occurred at the funeral of a teenager when family and friends painted the pine box that was to carry him to the crematorium. The act of painting the box helped people process this sudden and untimely death and feel that they were each personally contributing to his loving tribute.

The Greeting: Ask a few friends or neighbors to act as greeters. It makes people feel comfortable and helps relieve nervousness to be personally welcomed. The greeters also can help anyone who needs special help. This personal welcome opens the possibility for a stronger heart connection among participants. The more comfortable everyone is with one another, the deeper you will be able to go in the ritual.

At this time give each guest a program, ask him to sign the guest book, or paint her name on a rock, or write a heart-felt message or whatever you have decided. Invite them to find a comfortable place to sit. You might want to have music playing as people arrive. You can choose a particular piece of music that the person loved or a classical piece like Handel's *Water Music* or Pachelbel's *Canon in D.*

Grounding and Centering: It is important to have a clear beginning to the ritual itself. Call everyone together and set the tone for the ceremony. Let the mourners know how the ritual will unfold and the opportunities for their participation. Give your guests permission to participate at the level at which they are comfortable. People need to know it is fine to be part of the service in any way they want, including being silent.

Ask the guests to place both feet on the ground, close their eyes, and take some slow deep breaths. Guide them in a short exercise to help them let go of their day-to-day lives and come fully into the present moment. Say a prayer or lead a meditation that speaks to the purpose of being together.

Creating a Sacred Space: To symbolically separate this time of gathering from the ordinary time in our lives, children might scatter flower petals or drop white stones around the outside of the circle. Or request that each person stand and turn to his neighbor and take her hand. Or ask each person to place a flower in the center of the circle, in a sense saying, "I am present and here to honor this life that has passed." These acts mark the beginning of the ritual and are our cue to enter a deeper mode of awareness.

An essential part of creating a sacred space is to invoke Spirit, God, Mother Goddess, or whatever image or deity is appropriate. It is the act of invoking Spirit that allows us to recognize the interconnectedness of all life, which opens the way to transformation. This is the time to ask for guidance to help open our hearts so that we may grieve well and help the deceased on his journey.

Sharing/Heart Connection: When a death occurs, it stirs up the mysteries of life and death. We feel death close to us and find ourselves grappling with questions about the meaning of life and death and searching for light in the darkness. Through prayer, poetry, and song we can begin to touch the places in ourselves that are difficult to express and to come to terms with our loss. During this part of the ritual, the eulogy is given. In a small group, you may wish to open this up and invite individuals to come forward and share their stories, memories, and thoughts about the person being remembered.

As each speaker finishes, the mourners may feel a need to acknowledge what has been said with applause. This is not appropriate in this setting and can best be handled by asking everyone to repeat a word or two after each speaker. Different traditions have used different words. In the Judeo-Christian tradition, they use "Amen." In many goddess-based religions, "Blessed Be" is said. In some Native American traditions, they follow with the word, "Ho." People can choose a phrase that feels most comfortable to them. This brings everyone into the ritual, even those who have chosen not to share.

In a larger group, due to time constraints, you will want to structure the sharing more by asking one or two people to speak, or if you want group participation, ask for a couple of words. For example, you can pass candles out to everyone and place a large candle in the front of the room. Ask each person to come forward in turn and light their small candle from the larger one. When they light their candle they can say one to three words to describe the deceased, such as, "great generous heart," "mischievous sprite," "brilliant negotiator," "she-bear," or whatever comes to mind. This creates a beautiful word painting of the many facets of the person. The candles can then be set upon the altar.

Another way to handle this is to ask each person to repeat the phrase "I remember him for his…" then add a word or two such as, "I remember him for his frankness," "I remember him for his outrageous story-telling," etc. A similar ceremony can be done with flowers. Baskets of hardy flowers with stems (daisies, marigolds, snapdragons, etc.) are passed around the room and everyone is asked to take one. Then as each person comes to the front, offering words as suggested above, he or she weaves the flower into a large wreath made out of grapevines or a heart or other form made out of chicken wire or some similar material. The flowers cover the wire and fill the form creating a colorful memorial piece.

In a very large group, you may want to lead a prayer that brings together what has just been expressed in the stories and poems. Then give everyone an opportunity to offer a personal prayer silently.

If you feel a more elaborate approach is right for the ceremony and you have a few days to prepare, you could put together a slide show of the individual during different phases of her life. This can be incredibly moving.

Sending Blessings/Letting Go: Now we reach the part of the ritual where the final good-byes are said. This is the time for scattering the ashes or planting a tree in honor of your loved one.

If you are planting a tree, rose bush, or creating a memorial garden, the mourners can step forward one at a time to plant their flower or place their painted rock around the tree or at the edge of the flower garden. They can say their personal good-byes or prayers at this time. Remember to give people permission to offer their prayers in silence.

A candle-lighting ceremony can be used toward the end of the program as a way to involve everyone in saying good-bye. Each person is passed an unlit candle. A family member lights the first candle and the flame is passed from person to person until all the candles are lit. These can then be placed in candleholders or in a basin of sand on the altar. Or the candle-lighting ceremony can be held outside by a pool or a pond and the guests could light floating candles as they express their good-byes.

Other ways to involve everyone are by sprinkling flower petals into or over the coffin or grave, by writing farewells in the sand at the edge of the sea, or by tossing colored stones into a pond. You might light a bonfire and have each person add a stick or a pinecone. Another idea is to ask the participants to write messages on colorful pieces of ribbon at the beginning of the ceremony and tie them to a tree that is to be planted over the grave. Other cultures have traditions you may wish to borrow, such as the Asian custom of burning paper money that is then floated off into a pond or lake in paper boats.

Use your imagination to guide you in creating a satisfying ending. A dramatic way to lift everyone's spirits at this time in the ritual is to release a dozen doves. A member of the family can release one dove and then the others are released in a flock slowly. At one ceremony, butterflies were released. Both of these rituals are very uplifting. You can find people who offer this service by talking to wedding planners or searching the Internet for wedding links.

Closing: A final prayer may be recited or the group may sing a closing song. This is also the time to give gratitude to Spirit for being present during the ritual, by saying something like, "Thank you, God (Mother Goddess, Great One), for being with us today and guiding us in honoring our beloved. May you watch over her and guide her on her journey. And may you continue to comfort us in the days ahead."

At the end, the guests will want to connect with each other. It is important to spend time together for support and healing. Invite everyone to share food, drink, and stories with the family. Stories told in an informal setting help to immortalize the memories. This is probably the only time a complete portrait of the person emerges. What better send off than to share these treasured stories? As it is said, "What is remembered, lives." Sharing food and drink together symbolizes the continuance of life and community.

Please remember that these suggestions are only guidelines. The important thing to keep in mind is to be authentic to the one you loved and to yourself. Create this important ceremony with honor and respect and an open heart.

Resources
and Recommended Reading

Organizations

Americans for Better Care of the Dying: P.O. Box 346, Marvin Center, Washington, DC 20052 (202) 530-9864 or www.abcd-caring.org

Chalice of Repose Project, Inc.: is a unique end-of-life patient care program and graduate level school of music-thanatology. It includes a palliative-clinical practice and an educational program. The Project, housed within St. Patrick Hospital, lovingly serves the spiritual and physical needs of the dying with prescriptive music and educates healthcare providers, the public, and clinicians. 312 East Pine Street, Missoula, MT 59802 (406) 329-2810 or www.Thanatologysaintpatrick.org

Choice in Dying, Inc.: Advocates for the right of dying patients to participate fully in decisions about their medical treatment at the end of life. It offers state-specific living wills and durable power of attorney forms. 200 Varick Street, New York, NY 10014 (800) 989-9455 or (212) 366-5540, ext. 242

CROSSINGS: Caring for Our Own at Death: A nonprofit charitable corporation, they provide education and inspirational materials for the renewal of in-home afterdeath care. Consultations, resource guide, seminars, and workshops. P.O. Box 721, Silver Spring, MD 20918 (301) 593-5451 or www.crossings.net

Funeral Consumers Alliance: Lisa Carlson, Director. The national organizations for 140 nonprofit societies, they play a major role in reforming the funeral industry. Assist members to locate low-cost mortuaries. Dedicated to a consumer's right to choose a meaningful, affordable, and dignified funeral. P.O. Box 10, Hinesburg, VT 05461 (800) 765-0107 or www.funerals.org

Home Funeral Ministry: Guides and supports families in practical matters should they choose to have a family directed funeral. Includes helping the family in filing necessary documentation, preparing the body for viewing, and assisting with transportation of the deceased at affordable rates. (707) 823-7709

Hospice Association of America: 228 7th Street, SE, Washington, DC 20003 (202) 546-4759 or www.hospice-america.org

Hospice Foundation of America: 2001 S Street NW, Suite 300, Washington, DC 20009 (800) 854-3402 or www.hospicefoundation.org

Living/Dying Project: Education and support for those who know they are dying and their caregivers. P.O. Box 357, Fairfax, CA 94978 (415) 456-3915 Dale Borglum, Director.

Memorial Ecosystems: Have created an innovative, economical, convenient, and mainstream choice for interment and look to become national leaders in providing socially and environmentally responsible death care services. 113 Retreat Street, Westminster, SC 29693 (864) 647-7798 or www.memorialecosystems.com

Midwest Bioethics Center: A community-based center that addresses ethical issues and works on issues such as advance care planning, patient rights, and managed care ethics with local, state, and national organizations. 1021-1025 Jefferson St., Kansas City, MO 64105 Rachel Reed, Communications Director. www.midbio.org

Missoula Demonstration Project: Fosters a community where people experience meaning at the end of life and have their healthcare choices honored. They are developing models for other communities nationwide. They host community forums, work with schools, and develop study groups. Barbara Spring, Ph.D., Director of Community Engagement, 320 East Main St., Missoula, MT 59802. (406) 728-1613 or www.missoulademonstration.org

National Hospice Organization: Aids families in caring for their dying at home. 1901 N. Moore Street, Suite 901, Arlington, VA 22209 (800) 658-8898 or www.nho.org

National Consumers League: 1701 K Street NW, Suite 1200, Washington, DC 20006 (202) 835-3323 or www.ncinet.org

Natural Death Care Project: An educational nonprofit organization that educates people about their rights in funeral choices and helps plan family-directed and at-home funerals including how to file papers. Separate manuals or a complete resource guide in binder form available. P.O. Box 1721, Sebastopol, CA 95473 (707) 824-0268 or www.naturaldeathcare.org

The Natural Death Centre: An educational charity that offers information on Green, inexpensive funerals and in-depth consumers' perspectives on the funeral trade. A society for home deaths

dedicated to improving the quality of living and dying.
20 Heber Road, London NW2 6AA, England 44-181-208-2853 or
www.newciv.org/GIB/death

Partnership for Caring: America's Voices for the Dying: 1035 30th
Street NW, Washington, DC 20007 (202) 296-8071 or
www.partnershipforcaring.org

Project on Death in America Open Society Institute: Promoting
excellence in end-of-life care. Focuses on medical, educational, and gov-
ernmental agencies. 400 West 59th Street, New York, NY 10019 or
www.soros.org/death

Rigpa Fellowship: Spirtual Care Education and Training Program:
Sogyal Rinpoche's teaching program, courses and audio tapes.
449 Powell Street, San Francisco, CA 94102 (415) 392-2055 or
www.atlantech.net/rigpa

Upaya: The Project on Being with Dying: Joan Halifax, founding
director. Model project that offers professional training programs,
retreats, educational materials. Consults nationally with individuals
and centers on spiritually assisted dying. 1404 Cerro Gordo Road,
Santa Fe, NM, 87501 (505) 986-8518 or www.rt.66/com/~upaya

Visiting Nurse Associations of America: 11 Beacon Street, Suite 910,
Boston, MA 02108 (617) 523-4042 or www.vnaa.org

Wilderness Rites: Earth-Based Healing Practices: Anne Stine,
Founder and Director, 20 Spring Grove Ave., San Rafael, CA 94901
(415) 457-3691 or www.wildernessrites.com

Zen Hospice Project: Founding director, Frank Ostaseski. Model
project that combines practical, emotional, and spiritual support for

AIDS and cancer patients. Provides education for the public and health professionals and offers consulting services for those who wish to develop hospice programs. 273 Page Street, San Francisco, CA 94102 (415) 863-2910 or www.zenhospice.org

Books

Albom, Mitch. *Tuesdays with Morrie: An Old Man, a Young Man, and Life's Greatest Lesson*. NY: Doubleday, 1997

Anderson, Patricia. *All of Us: Americans Talk About the Meaning of Death*. NY: Delacorte Press, 1996

Bennett, Amanda and Terence B. Foley. *In Memoriam, A Practical Guide to Planning a Memorial Service*. NY: Simon & Schuster, 1997

Bly, Robert. *A Little Book on the Human Shadow*. San Francisco: HarperCollins, 1992

Bauby, Jean-Dominique. *The Diving Bell and the Butterfly*. NY: Vintage Books, 1998

Byock, Ira, M.D. *Dying Well: the Prospect for Growth at the End of Life*. NY: Riverhead Books, 1998

Carlson, Lisa. *Caring for the Dead: Your Final Act of Love. Hinesburg*, VT: Upper Access Books, 1998

Colgrove, Melba, Peter McWilliams, and Harold H. Bloomfield. *How to Survive the Loss of a Love*. Los Angeles, CA: Prelude Press, 1993

Cooper, Rabbi David A. *God Is a Verb*. NY: Penguin, 1998

Despelder, Lynne Ann and Albert Lee Strickland, eds. *The Last Dance: Encountering Death and Dying.* Mountain View, CA: Mayfield Publishing, 1999

Duda, Deborah. *Coming Home: A Guide to Dying at Home with Dignity.* NY: Aurora Press, 1987

Gill, Sue and John Fox. *The Dead Good Funerals Book.* Engineers of the Imagination. Distributed by Edge of Time Ltd, P.O. Box 1808, Winslow, Buckingham, MK 18 3 RN, 07000 780536.

H. H. the Dalai Lama. *The Joy of Living and Dying in Peace.* San Francisco: HarperCollins, 1997

Hogan, Pat. *Alison's Gift: The Song of a Thousand Hearts Opening.* Silver Spring, MD: NOSILA Publishing, 1999

Iserson, Kenneth V., M.D. *Dust to Dust.* Tucson, AZ: Galen Press, 1995

Jung, Carl Gustav. *The Undiscovered Self: With Symbols and the Interpretations of Dreams.* Princeton, NJ: Princeton University Press, 1990

Kelerman, Stanley. *Living Your Dying.* Berkeley, CA: Center Press, 1983.

Kornfield, Jack. *A Path with Heart: A Guide Through the Perils and Promises of Spiritual Life.* NY: Bantam, Doubleday, Dell, 1993

Kübler-Ross, Elizabeth. *On Death and Dying.* NY: Simon & Schuster, 1997

Kübler-Ross, Elizabeth. *Remember the Secret.* Berkeley, CA: Celestial Arts, 1998

Levine, Stephen. *A Year to Live: How to Live This Year As If It Were Your Last.* NY: Bell Tower, 1997

Levine, Stephen. *Who Dies? An Investigation of Conscious Living and Conscious Dying.* NY: Doubleday, 1982

Longaker, Christine. *Facing Death and Finding Hope: A Guide to the Emotional and Spiritual Care of the Dying.* NY: Doubleday, 1997

Miller, Sukie, Ph.D. *After Death: Mapping the Journey.* NY: Simon & Schuster, 1997

Mitford, Jessica. *The American Way of Death Revisited.* NY: Alfred A. Knopf, 1998

Morgan, Ernest. *Dealing Creatively with Death; A Manual of Death Education & Simple Burial.* Hinesburg, VT: Upper Access Books, 2000

Murray, Elizabeth. *Cultivating Sacred Space: Gardening for the Soul.* Rohnert Park, CA: Pomegranate, 1997

Nhat Hanh, Thich. *Being Peace.* Berkeley, CA: Parallax Press, 1987

Nearing, Helen. *Loving and Leaving the Good Life.* Post Mills, VT: Chelsea Green Publishing Company, 1992

Nuland, Dr. Sherwin. *How We Die: Reflections on Life's Final Chapter.* NY: Alfred A. Knopf, 1994

Palmer, Greg. *Death: The Trip of a Lifetime.* San Francisco: HarperCollins, 1993

Rinpoche, Sogyal. *The Tibetan Book of Living and Dying.* San Francisco: HarperCollins, 1993

Shaw, Eva. *What to do When a Loved One Dies: A Practical and Compassionate Guide to Dealing with Death on Life's Terms.* Irving, CA: Dickens Press, 1994

Singh, Kathleen D. *The Grace in Dying: How We are Transformed Spiritually as We Die.* San Francisco: HarperCollins, 1998

Some, Malidoma Patrice. *Ritual: Power, Healing and Community.* NY: Penguin, 1997

Starhawk, M. Mach Nightmare, and the Reclaiming Collective. *The Pagan Book of Living and Dying: Practical Rituals, Prayers, Blessings, and Meditations on Crossing Over.* San Francisco: HarperCollins, 1997

Webb, Marilyn. *The Good Death: The New American Search to Reshape the End of Life.* NY:Doubleday, 1999

Self-help Legal Information:

Books

All from Nolo.com. 950 Parker St., Berkeley, CA 94710 (800) 992-6656 or www.nolo.com

Clifford, Denis and Mary Randolph. *9 Ways to Avoid Estate Taxes: The Best Guide to Keeping Your Estate from the Tax Man* and *Estate Planning Basics: What You Need to Know and Nothing More*

Randolph, Mary. *8 Ways to Avoid Probate: Save Your Family Thousands of Dollars.*

Books Including Forms and a CD

Clifford, Denis. *Will Book* and *Make Your Own Living Trust*

Computer Programs

WillMaker and *Living Trust Maker*

Heirloom Memory Books

Lomasney, Maureen. *My Life: Truth, Tales, Memories and Dreams.* Tannery Creek Press, Box 221, Graton, CA 95444

McPhelimy, Lynn. *In the Checklist of Life: A Working Book to Help You Live and Leave This Life!* AAIP Publishing Co., P.O. Box 102, Rockfall, CT 06481

Wiard, Warren L. *Living Memories/Loving Memories.* Jean Barnes Books, 2717 NW 50th, Oklahoma City, OK 73117

Preserving Family Histories

Sojourna Productions: Will help you revisit and preserve family and personal stories through book, video, or CD format. They also offer workshops in writing an ethical will and creating your own memorial or bereavement book. 708 Gravenstein Hwy North, P.M.B. #100, Sebastopol, CA 95472 (707) 829-3900 or www.sojourna.com

Publications

Before I Go, You Should Know. End-of-life planning kit in a plastic pouch. Illustrations by Edward Gorey. Includes state-specific Living Will and other advance directives and a 20-page booklet to write in other important information. Fill it out, store in your refrigerator or freezer, and put the enclosed magnet on the door to alert your family and friends. Available from your local funeral/memorial society. Check the phone book or contact the Funeral Consumers Alliance, P.O. Box 10, Hinesburg, VT 05461 (800) 765-0107 or www.funerals.org

Body and Organ Donation. Free brochure on becoming an organ or tissue donor. 800-888-55-74273

CRITICAL Conditions Planning Guide. Helps families and individuals make final healthcare decisions. Georgia Health Decisions. (877) 633-2433 or

Finding Your Way: A Guide for End-of-Life Medical Decisions. Sacramento Healthcare Decisions. (916) 484-2485 or www.sachealthdecisions.org

Funeral Goods and Services. The American Association of Retired Persons (AARP), 601 E Street NW, Washington, DC 20049

A Guide to Recalling and Telling Your Life Story. Hospice foundation of America. (800) 854-3402 or www.hospicefoundation.org

Light in the Mist. Healing Environments (Creating Poetic Spaces for Healing) 451 Lytton Ave., Palo Alto, CA 94301 (650) 322-1428 or www.Healingenvironments.org Gives comfort to patients, their families, and caregivers by connecting them to the transforming power of the arts.

Talking it Over: A Guide for Group Discussions on End-of-Life Decisions. Sacramento Healthcare Decisions. (916) 484-2485 www.sachealthdecisions.org

Audio

Levine, Stephen and Ondrea. *Grief Meditation, Healing into Life and Death, Conscious Living/Conscious Dying* and many others. Video tapes also available.

Warm Rock Tapes. P.O. Box 108, Chamisal, NM 87521, (800) 731-4325

Halifax, Joan, Ph.D. *Being with Dying.* Set of six tapes incorporating meditation and philosophy to help prepare for an aware and mindful death.

Stephen Levine, Joan Halifax, Ram Dass, Rachel Naomi Remen, Sogyal Rinpoche, and others also available from **Sounds True,** 413 S. Arthur Avenue, Louisville, CO 80027 (800) 333-9185 or www.SoundsTrue.com

Video

Kaufman, Paul and Jennifer. *Chalice of Repose: A Contemplative Musician's Approach to Death and Dying with Therese Schroeder-Shecker.* **Sounds True.** This documentary chronicles the lives of the musicians and the patients who have had their pain eased through music.

Moyers, Bill and Judith. *On Our Own Terms: Moyers on Dying.* Films of the Humanities (800) 257-5126 Four-part, six-hour series chronicles the intimate stories of patients and their families as they struggle to balance medical intervention with comfort and compassion at the end of life.

Coffins and Urns

Artful Life & Death: Includes workshops on coffin and urn painting, ceramic funeral wreaths, shrine making, and life passage ceremonies. Carole Rae Watanabe and Salli Rasberry. Box 146 Bodega, CA, 94922 www.artfully.com

Casket Gallery Showrooms, Funeral & Cremation Advisory Centers: Urns from around the world and clothwood caskets. Shipping around the U.S. within 24 hrs. Full Spanish-speaking staff. 1027 Broadway Ave., El Cajon, CA 92021 (619) 444-4442 or 888-782-2753

Casket Outlet: Discount funeral home caskets. Storage free for first year. 584 Grand Ave., Oakland, CA 94610 (510) 893-6550

Craig Convissor: Caskets and cremation urns. Plain pine or hardwood handcrafted memorials: crosses, benches, flower stands. 5583 Bancroft SE, Alto, MI 49302 (616) 868-6925

Cumberland Woodworks: Amish/Mennonite coffins. Native American hardwoods. Box 162B Altamount, TN 37301 (615) 692-2369

Florette & Robert Dorr: Wood urns for pet and human remains. 151 The Great Rd., Groton, VT 05046 (800) 228-4021

Grinnell Coffin Works: Plywood, pine and native hardwood
502 4th Ave., Grinnell, IA 50112 (515) 236-4662

Mineral Crossing of the West: Softwood caskets. 1416 Palmer Dr.
Laramie, WY 82070 (307) 745-6915

Morris Bridge Coffin Co.: Softwood/hardwood, artistic personalizing
available. 15801 Morris Bridge Rd., Tampa, FL 33592
(813) 986-7574

Norwal Unltd.: Terra cotta and glazed urns. P.O. Box 547,
Alfred Station, NY 14803 (607) 587-9566

Plain Pine Boxes: Inexpensive coffins, caskets, and urns. Box 1307,
Forestville, CA 95436 (707) 578-7709

Pine Box Handcrafted Coffins: Custom made wide-shouldered
coffins. 2403 N. Logan Ave., Colorado Springs, CO 80907
(719) 329-1139

Rare Earth: Spirit urns. Don Watanabe 740 Pine Crest Ave.,
Sebastopol, CA, 95422 (707) 823-9663 or www.artfully.com

Relict Memorials: This studio offers a unique form of memorial that
includes the cremated remains as an integral part of a dignified and
classically simple tablet. This tablet safely contains the remains and
provides for *custom memorial recognition*; it can be readily relocated
and will endure for generations.1050 Redwood Hwy, Mill Valley,
CA 94941 (800) 381-6536 or www.relicts.com

Zwisler Bros. Handrafted Wood Products: Oak and aspen, finished
or unfinished, lined or unlined, kit or assembled. P.O. Box 200,
Bayfield, CO 81122 (800) 621-4992

About the Authors

Salli Rasberry

Best selling author Salli Rasberry helped lead the back-to-the-land movement in the late 60s. Her books on education, money, business, and creativity provided inspiration and guidance to a generation of modern pioneers. She has lived in a teepee, been a working partner on a sheep ranch, started an alternative school, and produced sex education films. An indefatigable activist, she now sings in the Threshold Choir, serves as president of the Sonoma Land Trust, and is on the board of the Redwood Funeral Society. An avid flower gardener and voracious environmentalist, she lives with her family in the rolling hills of western Sonoma County, California.

Carole Rae Watanabe

Always recognized as being ahead of her time, Carole has transformed the art landscape of the Bay Area with such innovative ideas as the first gallery for the fiber arts, the Danger Rangers, and the Apprentice Alliance. She has now turned her irrepressible energy to southern France, where she has created Art Heaven in a medieval village. Her paintings, sculptural paper works, and tapestries are held in private and public collections throughout the world.